SHERRY SERAFINI'S

SENSATIONAL BEAD EMBROIDERY

SHERRY SERAFINI'S

SENSATIONAL BEAD EMBROIDERY

25 INSPIRING JEWELRY PROJECTS

An Imprint of Sterling Publishing Co., Inc.
New York

WWW.LARKCRAFTS.COM

Editor
Nathalie Mornu

Development Editor
Ray Hemachandra

Technical Editor
Judith Durant

Art Director
Carol Morse Barnao

Editorial Assistance
Abby Haffelt

Illustrators
J'aime Allene and Bonnie Brooks

Photography Director
Kathleen Holmes

Photographer
Stewart O'Shields

Cover Designer
Kathleen Holmes

Library of Congress Cataloging-in-Publication Data

Serafini, Sherry.
 [Sensational bead embroidery]
 Sherry Serafini's sensational bead embroidery : 25 inspiring jewelry projects / Sherry Serafini.
   p. cm.
 Includes index.
 ISBN 978-1-60059-672-8 (hc-plc : alk. paper)
 1. Beadwork. 2. Embroidery. I. Title. II. Title: Sensational bead embroidery.
 TT860.S47 2011
 746.5--dc22

                                        2010032948

10 9 8 7 6 5 4 3 2 1

First Edition

Published by Lark Crafts, An Imprint of Sterling Publishing Co., Inc.
387 Park Avenue South, New York, NY 10016

Text © 2011, Sherry Serafini
Photography © 2011, Lark Crafts, An Imprint of Sterling Publishing Co., Inc., unless otherwise specified
Illustrations © 2011, Lark Crafts, An Imprint of Sterling Publishing Co., Inc., unless otherwise specified

Distributed in Canada by Sterling Publishing,
c/o Canadian Manda Group, 165 Dufferin Street
Toronto, Ontario, Canada M6K 3H6

Distributed in the United Kingdom by GMC Distribution Services,
Castle Place, 166 High Street, Lewes, East Sussex, England BN7 1XU

Distributed in Australia by Capricorn Link (Australia) Pty Ltd.,
P.O. Box 704, Windsor, NSW 2756 Australia

If you have questions or comments about this book, please contact:
Lark Crafts, 67 Broadway, Asheville, NC 28801
828-253-0467

Manufactured in China

ISBN 13: 978-1-60059-672-8

For information about custom editions, special sales, and premium and corporate purchases, please contact the Sterling Special Sales Department at 800-805-5489 or specialsales@sterlingpub.com.

For information about desk and examination copies available to college and university professors, submit requests to academic@larkbooks.com. Our complete policy can be found at www.larkcrafts.com.

CONTENTS

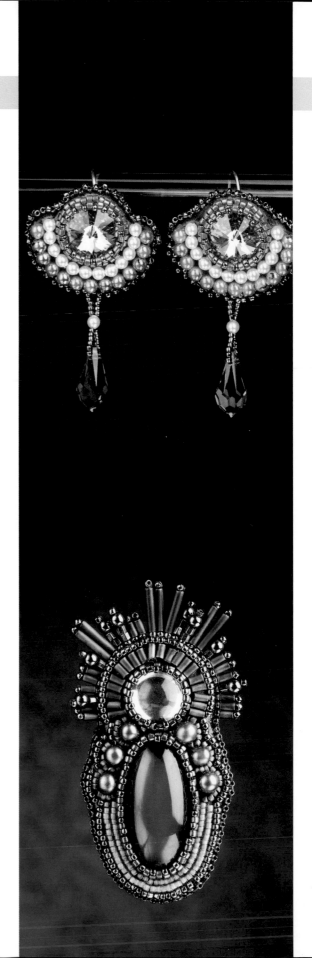

INTRODUCTION

I'VE EXPLORED JUST ABOUT EVERY MEDIUM ON THE PLANET.

I have a degree in graphic design and studied fine art in college, and fine beadwork always interested me. When I decided to give beading a try, the tiny glass treasures instantly mesmerized me. I tried my hand at various beading stitches and found myself drawn to embroidery stitches using cabochons as focal points. Because it doesn't require much planning ahead, there's so much freedom in bead embroidery, and *that* is perfect for the creative restless soul.

This medium is wonderful if you desire spontaneity in your designs. While bead embroidery can start from specific patterns with specific bead placements, there's also the option of being completely impromptu with the beads you choose to use. It's sometimes fun to just glue down a cabochon or button on the middle of a large piece of foundation and, with no other plan in mind, let the focal bead tell you what the final piece of jewelry wants to be by messing around with bead placement.

In this book, I'll take you step by step through my approach to stitches and design. Some projects, like Give Me a Ring (page 62), will be very simple, while others, such as the Rockin' Wavy Cuff (page 103), will challenge your design sense and force you to think outside the box. The techniques I introduce you to include peyote stitch, single-bead edging, and basic embroidery stitches. You'll combine these to create the 25 wearable pieces of art for which I give you step-by-step instructions. These include rings, brooches, necklaces, and bracelets. I also devote a page to sharing my approach to design and color.

A grand part of our fun will be choosing the cabochons, pins, buttons, and beads that you get to play with and then turn into a project (and quite possibly not the one you originally envisioned!). While you may not be able to locate the exact items I use in my projects, you can substitute with minimal change. Your 18-mm round stone may be blue while mine was purple, for example, or you might have a different button, natural stone, or brass finding. Once again, that's the freedom and beauty of bead embroidery, and I encourage you to get excited and find your creative voice.

I've written this book with the intent of stirring your imagination. I created these projects for you, and I hope they inspire you and guide you down your own path. In these pages, I give you basic ground rules and stitches to explore, and with those, there's no limit to where your imagination can take you. I hope you'll find your inner artist and not only master the stitches, but have some fun creating from your heart. I challenge you to become the creator, to let your own vision and inner voice take over while you make your own one-of-a-kind bead embroidered jewelry.

CHAPTER ONE
BASIC MATERIALS
AND TOOLS

There's no end to the types of beads and findings you can use for your bead embroidery. Here are the materials used for the projects presented in this book.

Cabochons

Cabochons take center stage in my embroidery. A cab (as they're sometimes called) is any object with a flat back and a domed surface. These can be round, square, oval, or irregular in shape. I usually glue cabs to a foundation with industrial strength adhesive and then peyote stitch a bezel around them. I try to keep my bezels in even-count peyote, though an odd count is often necessary with a freeform shape.

Stones

Natural stone cabochons are often one-of-a-kind, so by using them, your piece automatically becomes unique. Stones can be very regular in shape, but there are also tons of gorgeous freeform natural stones available.

Buttons

Buttons make wonderful focal points! Simply use wire cutters to cut the shank off the back of a button and it becomes an instant cabochon. The exception would be a glass button that has a shank that can't be removed; these can be treated the same as rivolis (next column). Acrylic and plastic buttons with simple pin backs can also be used. Just pull the pin back out and glue the button to the foundation.

Rivolis and Pointed-Back Stones

Rivolis are faceted crystal rhinestones with a point on the back. A strong beading foundation can turn any pointed-back stone into an instant cabochon. Refer to page 21 in chapter 2 for details.

Seed Beads

I use a wide variety of glass seed beads, from size 15° (small) to size 6° (large). Cylinder beads are seed beads with thin walls and large holes that come in sizes 15°, 11°, 10°, and 8°. Seed beads come in a variety of colors and finishes including matte, metallic, iris, Aurora Borealis (AB), luster, transparent, lined, and opaque. Placing beads with different finishes next to each other adds dimension to your beadwork. Mixing them to make a bead soup is a great way to use up the leftovers you just don't want to part with.

Fun Beads

I call the extra elements I use around my seed beads fun beads. Round and seed pearls, round and bicone crystals, short and long bugle beads, fire-polished Czech beads, and various odd-shaped beads can be used in your embroidered projects. They all lend texture and interest to a design.

Beading Foundation

I use a special beading foundation material called Lacy's Stiff Stuff. It comes in 8½ x 11-inch (21.6 x 27.9 cm) sheets and is available on the Internet and in tons of beading stores. Created specifically for cabochon use and for bead embroidery, it's durable and can be dyed with fabric dye and painted with acrylics—I've even washed it, and it survived the torture! My biggest argument for this material is that it doesn't fray, which is very important for my edging techniques. Unless I'm doing a piece with light-colored beads, I like to dye my foundation gray/black, which allows the beads to shine in the forefront with the foundation fading into the background.

Synthetic Suede

Use synthetic suede, often marketed under the name Ultrasuede, to back your finished pieces. It comes in a wide variety of colors, which makes it great for matching your beadwork. It's also lightweight, which makes it easy for the needle to glide through when working the edges of a design. The fabric can also be left peeking through on some projects and used as a backdrop for the beads.

Findings

A number of findings are used in the projects presented in this book; they turn beadwork into jewelry.

Earring Findings

French ear wires, or fish-hook ear wires, have a loop that holds the bead-work and a U-shaped hook that fits into your lobe. The wire often has a coil or a bead between the loop and the hooked part that goes into the ear.

Post earring findings have a flat back with a single post protruding from the center. A backing fits over the post to create an earring that fits tightly against your ear lobe. These are available with flat fronts onto which you can glue your beadwork.

Closures and Clasps

I like bar clasps for closures on bracelets. One side of the clasp slides inside the other and locks into place. My beadwork is very busy, so keeping the closure simple is my chosen method.

Another very simple closure that works well is the hook and eye, like those used on clothing. These are stitched to the back side of the beadwork, and the stitching is covered by the suede backing.

Toggle clasps are available in a wide variety of styles. From the vintage to the modern, your choices are endless. They make wonderful simple closures for necklaces.

Bar pins are sized anywhere from ¾ to 2 inches (1.9 to 5.1 cm) in length. Glue them to the back of beadwork to make brooches.

Metal Blanks

Raw metal blanks are used between the beadwork and the suede when an unbendable foundation is desired. I use these for cuffs and rings.

Needles

I use sizes 10, 11, and 13 longs to work with a wide variety of beads. Sometimes switching needles in the middle of a project is imperative; a freshwater pearl may have a hole that won't accommodate the larger needle I've been working with. Never force a needle through a bead, because it might break the bead.

Thread

There are many wonderful beading threads available and I usually tell my students to choose their favorite. For embroidery I use nylon thread, and my preference is Nymo B (lighter) for the smallest beads or D (heavier) for larger beads. I sometimes use a heavier weight braided beading thread called Fireline that was originally developed for fishing. It has become a favorite of beaders, especially when backstitching crystals or beads with sharp edges that may fray nylon beading thread. Use your favorite threads and pay more attention to the color than the brand. If you plan to back a piece with suede, it's very important to match the thread color to the suede.

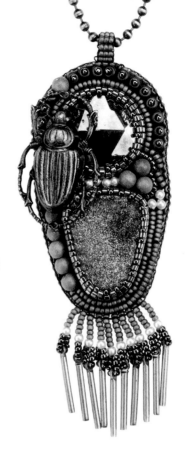

Scissors

You *have* to have good scissors! Dedicate a small sharp pair to your beadwork and your beadwork only, to use for cutting and snipping nylon thread. Using this pair on other items such as paper or braided beading thread will ruin it—don't do it. Buy a separate pair of inexpensive craft scissors for cutting braided beading thread and paper.

Thread Burner

We'll be clipping a lot of threads close to the beadwork, and it's often impossible to get that wee little pesky piece with scissors. A thread burner is great for getting rid of these bits, and its precision tip won't affect the rest of the beadwork.

Adhesives

Adhesives are used in a variety of ways with bead embroidery.

Industrial Strength Adhesive

An industrial-strength adhesive permanently holds cabochons in place, and I prefer E6000. Available through craft and beading stores, this stuff is fabulous for attaching your cabochons or findings when you're not stitching a bezel around them. Always use adhesives in a well-ventilated area, and don't inhale the fumes. Read the labels for safety warnings and follow them. If you're going to bezel around a cabochon, it's not necessary to use the industrial strength, but it doesn't hurt.

Double-Sided Tape

A good industrial-strength, double-sided tape is great for holding stones or buttons in place while you work. However, I don't recommend this material unless you're going to create a bezel around the stone—glue is my choice for long-lasting hold.

White Glue

Thick and tacky white craft glue is user friendly. I use it to adhere suede to beadwork for finishing. There's no need for industrial-strength adhesive in the final steps. However, I never use this on cabochons; it just doesn't hold.

Toothpicks and Dowels

Wooden toothpicks and small wooden dowels make handy tools for spreading adhesive in thin layers over the backs of beadwork, suede, or metal blanks.

Paper

You'll use 8½ x 11-inch (21.6 x 27.9 mm) sheets of plain white paper to create patterns before you start beading.

Ruler

A ruler is helpful in determining centers of cuffs and for setting guidelines within which to bead.

Marking Tools

Pencils come in handy for sketching out design ideas. Permanent markers are essential in my beadwork. I keep several colors with different points, with the fine point being the most useful. It comes in handy for drawing designs or making guidelines for an asymmetrical piece. I use a permanent marker because I don't want the marks to rub off on my beads. You can also use markers on the edges of beading foundation if you don't want the white showing.

Task Lamp

Good lighting is a must! I prefer the natural light that comes in from my kitchen windows, where my studio is. However, that's not always the place that I bead, so I carry a task lamp with me for such occasions. There are a lot of wonderful, transportable lamps available that provide lighting for your art making regardless of where you are.

Optional Tools

Some projects require a few additional tools, and these will be listed in the supply list only when they're necessary.

Poster Board

Poster board is used for added stiffness. I use it often for pendants and brooches and for any heavy piece of beadwork.

Protractor

This helps determine the proper sizes for shaped collars.

Wire Cutters

Used for cutting wires and snipping the shanks off buttons that are used as cabochons.

Pliers

Round-nose, flat-nose, and chain-nose pliers are used to form simple and wrapped loops from wire.

Templates

Good templates made of sturdy plastic are available at art or craft stores in the artists' supplies department. Available in square and round shapes of various widths and circumferences, they're great for creating perfectly shaped embroidered earrings.

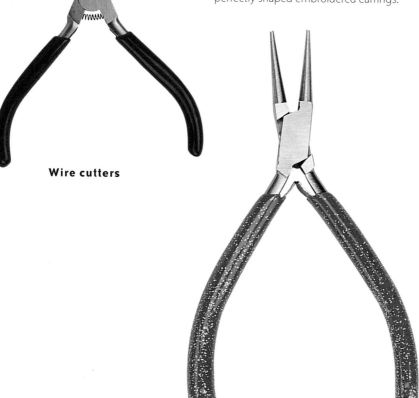

Wire cutters

Round-nose pliers

Crimpers

CHAPTER TWO

STITCHES AND GENERAL TECHNIQUES

As with other types of beadwork, bead embroidery uses specific stitches and other techniques. While there are many stitches that can be adapted to embroidery, these have become my favorites for enhancing focal points. Here's what you'll need to complete the projects presented in this book.

Two-Bead Backstitch

I use this stitch exclusively for embroidery because of the many curves in my patterns. It's the best way to keep the beads lying flat. I consider the beading foundation to be my canvas, with the beads as my paint. I don't want the "paint" to bubble up off the canvas in an unattractive manner. Stitching no more than two beads at a time allows them to be securely fastened to the canvas.

Using a single thread, knot the end. Pass your needle and thread up through the foundation next to a stone or wherever you are beginning your backstitch in the embroidery. Pick up 2 beads and pull them snug against the foundation, positioning them in the direction you want them to go. Pass the needle down through the foundation next to where the second bead rests, pulling all the thread and beads down tight. Pass the needle back up from the underside to where the first bead was strung and pass through both beads again (figure 1). Pick up 2 more beads, placing them snug against the first two that you started with. Come back up between the first and second beads, pass through the second, third, and fourth beads again, and string on 2 more beads (figure 2). You're essentially stringing on two, coming back through three.

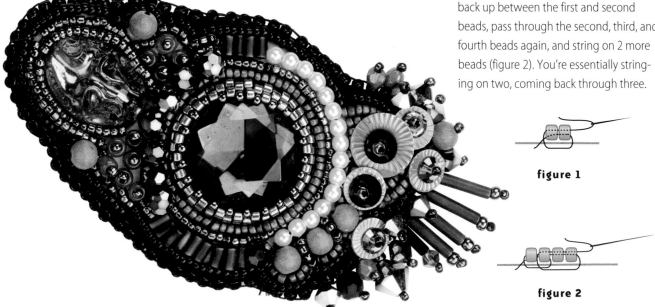

figure 1

figure 2

Sherry Serafini
Ferguson, 2004
76.2 x 19 cm
Assorted beads; embroidered

Even-Count Peyote Stitch in the Round

I prefer to work even-count peyote rather than odd-count peyote stitch, and I use it to create a bezel after an even number of beads has been backstitched around a cabochon.

Bring your needle straight up from underneath the foundation and pass it through 1 of the beads in the backstitched round. String a bead on the needle, skip the next bead in the base round, and pass the needle through the following bead (figure 3). Repeat this around the base round. To begin the next round of an even-count peyote stitch, step up by passing again through the first bead (figure 4). Pick up a new bead and continue around through all of the up beads, stepping up once again when you've reached the end of the working round.

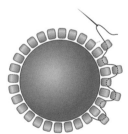

figure 3

figure 4

Odd-Count Peyote Stitch in the Round

Sometimes it's not possible to backstitch an even number of beads around odd shapes, so you have to use odd-count peyote to create a bezel. This is done exactly as even-count peyote stitch except that you don't have a step up at the end of the round. Upon completion of each round, you simply keep going into the next round.

Closing Up Around a Cabochon

To close up and tighten around your cabochons or buttons, use a smaller bead, like a size 15°, in the final row of peyote stitch. When the bezel starts to flare out, switch to the smaller beads (figure 5).

Single-Bead Edging

This stitch finishes the edges of the bead embroidery. It can be left as it is for a clean, finished edge, or you can add fringe or attachments to the open holes.

Single thread your needle and tie a knot at the end. Thread length will depend upon the size of the project, but you want enough thread to go around the entire project without rethreading. Weave the needle through the beadwork, hiding the knot under the beads or between the layers of suede and beadwork. Exit the top edge of the beadwork, and pick up a size 11° or 15° bead and sew up through

the foundation and the suede to attach. Before tightening the stitch, pass through the bead again (figure 6). Pull the thread taut (figure 7), then pick up another bead and repeat this step (figure 8).

Continue around the entire piece until your last bead meets your first. Pass the needle and thread down through the first bead stitched. Weave the needle and thread down through the beadwork on the design, tying off several times between the beads and hiding the knots. Clip the thread as close to the beadwork as possible.

figure 5

figure 6

figure 7

figure 8

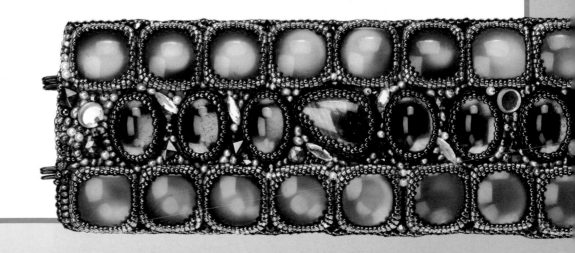

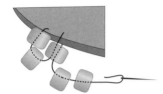

figure 9

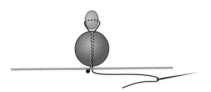

figure 10

figure 11

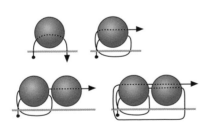

figure 12

figure 13

Picot Edging

Like the single-bead edging, this finishes the edges. The only difference: to create a picot edge, you pick up more beads in the stitch.

Anchor the thread as for single-bead edging, then pick up 3 beads (figure 9). Pass the needle up through the suede and the edge of the beadwork, then through the third bead again. Pass the needle back up through the third bead added and pull snug. Pick up 2 beads (figure 10), and pass down through the foundation and the suede once again, then bring the needle up through the second bead added. Continue around in this manner until your last bead meets your first. Pick up 1 bead and pass down through the first bead you began with and weave the needle through the beadwork, tying off knots like you did in the single-bead edging.

Stop Stitches

Pass the needle up from underneath the foundation. Pick up a large bead like a pearl, crystal, or size 6° or 8° seed bead. Pick up a smaller seed bead to be the stopper. Skip over the smaller bead and pass the needle down through the larger bead and the foundation (figure 11). Repeat this stitch for strength.

Embroidering with Specific Beads

Bugle beads should be sewn on one at a time. Because the bead holes can be sharp and could cut the thread, either sew through twice or sew with double thread. Adding a buffer bead on each side of the bugle is another option (figure 12).

4–6 mm round beads should be backstitched one at a time so that they lie flat against your foundation (figure 13).

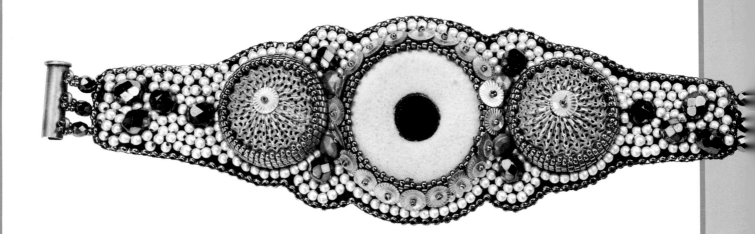

Czech beads and crystals are usually back-stitched one at a time so that one of the facets lies against the foundation. Crystal edges can be sharp, so be sure to stitch through at least twice or use buffer beads (figure 14).

I like to use sequins, rondelles, and other flat back beads as stop stitches (see previous page) on top of existing beadwork (figure 15). Stop stitches become top stitches when stitched on top of the beads. You can also use these to hide spaces between bugle beads.

Set rivolis into an extra layer of foundation to cushion the points. Trace around the stone where you want it to go on your foundation. Cut a small hole at the center of your traced design (figure 16)—start small and cut bigger if needed. You want the hole to accommodate the point on the back of the stone. Then simply glue the edges of the stone to the foundation and bezel around it to secure (figure 17).

Embellishing a Peyote-Stitch Bezel

I use this stitch for embellishment with a peyote-stitch bezel around a button or stone. Weave the needle through one of the beads in a chosen row of the peyote-stitch bezel. Pick up 1 bead, then pick up a smaller stop bead. Pass the needle back through the larger bead, then through the next bead in the row (figure 18).

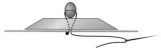

figure 14

figure 15

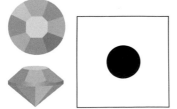
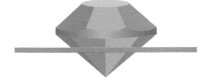
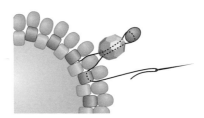

figure 16

figure 17

figure 18

Crosshatching

This is a simple but beautiful way to stitch beads in spaces that you want to fill up in a large embroidered piece. Working the two-bead backstitch, stitch 4 to 5 rows of 4 to 6 beads in one direction. Using the same color beads, switch directions and stitch 4 or 5 more rows (figure 19). Keep changing the direction of the beads and you will begin to see a pattern emerge. This stitch looks best when size 15° beads or smaller are used.

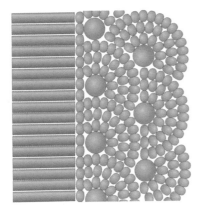

figure 19

Scalloping

Stitch a larger bead, like a 4- or 5-mm round, down onto your foundation. Backstitch a simple row of size 15°s around the bead. Backstitch two to three more rows around the first backstitched row. Stitch on another larger bead against the 15°s just stitched. Work a row of 15°s around this larger bead. Continue stitching in this manner and you'll see a pattern emerge in your design (figure 20). It's a great way to fill areas and add interest.

figure 20

figure 21

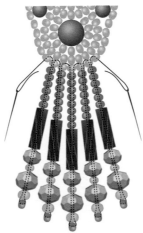

figure 22

Fringe and Attachments

You can pass the needle and thread through the edge beads to attach separate embroidered components, add fringe, and attach ear wires. These techniques are done after the pieces are completely beaded, backed with suede, and edged with single-bead edging.

Fringe

Fringe is attached through the single-bead edging. A double-needle method can be used on a large piece to ensure that the fringe is even on both sides. Using a wingspan length of thread or longer (do what's comfortable for you), add a needle to both ends. String on your center fringe row and pass both needles up through the bead at the center bottom edge of your beadwork (figure 21). Pass one needle down through the edge bead on the right side of the center and the other needle through the bead on the left side. You can now work each side simultaneously to make sure both sides are equal (figure 22).

A smaller piece can be worked with only one needle, like when you're just adding little spikes evenly the whole way around a piece or with random fringe.

Attaching Components

Embroidered components should be joined utilizing the single-bead edging techniques described in the stitch section. Simply add strands of beads between the pieces, working from edge bead to edge bead (figure 23). You can use as few as 3 beads for a pair of earrings, or a much larger quantity for a neckpiece (figure 24).

Ladder Stitch

I use this when creating a bail or a ring band. Locate the center top three beads of the single-bead edging and pass the needle and thread up through one of the beads on the right or left. Pick up 3 of the same size beads used in the edging and pass the needle and thread down through the edge bead on the opposite side. Weave the needle and thread back up through the edge bead you started with and pass through the 3 beads just added (figure 25). Pick up 3 more seed beads, pass back through the last row and again through the beads just added (figure 26). Repeat this procedure for the desired length of the bail. Connect the last row to the first and weave through twice for strength (figure 27). Weave down through an edge bead and into the embroidery, tying off with several small knots to secure.

Loops

To create a simple loop bail, locate the center top 3 beads of the single-bead edging, and pass the needle and thread up through one of the beads on the right or left. Pick up enough beads to create a large enough loop to go around the chosen rope or chain you want to use. Pass the needle and thread down through the same edge bead (figure 28). Pass up through the middle bead and repeat these steps. Pass through the third edge bead and repeat these steps again. Weave through all of the loops again for strength.

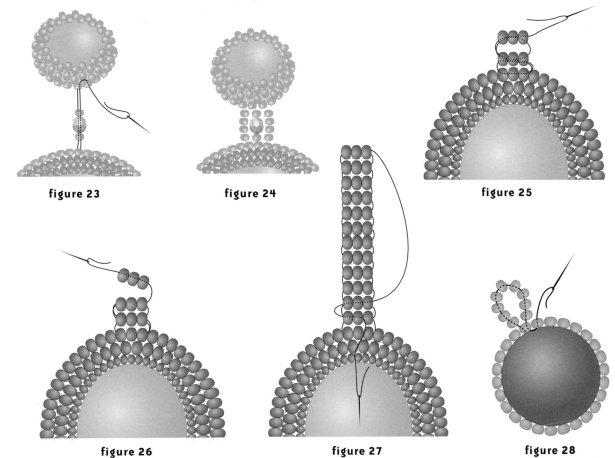

figure 23   figure 24   figure 25

figure 26   figure 27   figure 28

Beginning a Thread

Thread a needle with single or doubled thread and tie an overhand knot at the end, making sure that the knot is large enough that it won't pull through the foundation. Bring the thread up through the foundation where you want to begin beading.

Adding Thread

When your thread gets to be around 5 inches (12.7 cm) long, tie it off on the back of the piece, and clip the thread. Begin a new thread as described above, passing up through the foundation where you want to begin beading again.

Tying Off and Hiding Knots

Bead embroidery allows you the freedom to weave in and out of the beadwork, tying off and hiding overhand knots between the beads. To finish a thread, weave into the beadwork, tie off with a tiny overhand knot, and pull up snug to hide the knot. Repeat this a few times for added security, then clip the thread close.

Gluing

When gluing down cabochons or buttons, keep the glue from seeping out around the edges. If it does seep out, just clean it up before it dries. When gluing the beadwork to the suede, keep the glue away from the edges so it won't interfere with the needle and thread passing through the edges when you do the final stitches.

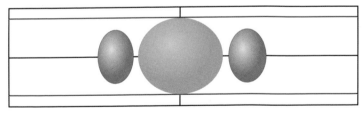

figure 29

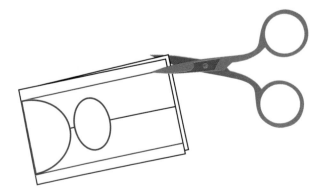

figure 30

Creating Patterns

Creating your own patterns is fun and easy. Draw them on plain white paper before you begin stitching.

Cuffs

Measure your wrist and cut the paper to the length desired, allowing enough length to include your chosen clasp. Determine from the focal point how wide you'd like the cuff to be. Cut this width out from the desired length of paper and use a ruler to draw lines at the vertical and horizontal centers of the paper. Put your focal bead and stones on the paper and trace around them (figure 29). If you want the cuff to be symmetrical on both sides, simply fold the paper in half and cut around the lines you've drawn (figure 30). Open the pattern up to view your symmetrical design and trace it onto the foundation. You can now glue your stones down to prepare for beading.

Collars

Use a protractor to draw a circle 5½ inches (14 cm) in diameter on a sheet of paper. This is the inner edge of your collar. Draw a vertical line through the center. Extend the line a few inches below the circle to delineate the center front. Measure 1 inch (2.5 cm) down from the top of the circle on the center line and make a mark. Draw a horizontal line through the circle at this mark. This line defines the neckpiece's back edges to achieve a curved fit. This size fits most necklines, but it certainly can be adjusted. Keep in mind that you'll be adding a clasp in the final stages and this will add about 2 inches (5.1 cm).

I often place the paper template around my own neck after cutting to see how it fits. If I find I'd like the neckpiece larger or smaller, I adjust the initial circumference.

Using your center mark as a guideline, draw your basic collar shape. Measure 1 to 1½ inches (2.5 to 3.8 cm) respectively from the center point (this will vary based on the size of the focal point), tapering to approximately ¼ inch (6.4 mm) wide in the back to accommodate your clasp (figure 31). Fold the paper in half on the center line. This will ensure that you're perfectly even on both sides of your template. Cut out the template and transfer it onto a sheet of foundation by using a permanent marker to trace around the perimeters of the pattern (figure 32).

Note: After a pattern's been traced onto the foundation, I generally don't cut on this line. I like to leave at least a ¼-inch (6.4 mm) margin the whole way around for several reasons:

• When doing your embroidery, it's easier if you have a little bit of an edge to hold on to.

• Waiting to cut means you'll have a slight bit of material that will accommodate a beaded edging. If you cut out beforehand, your design will be stitched right to the edge, leaving no room for finishing.

• Designs change! I don't cut on the line because in the middle of a design I may change directions. For example, my first collar began as a brooch that started on an 8½ x 11-inch (21.6 x 27.9 cm) sheet of foundation fabric. It grew as I beaded!

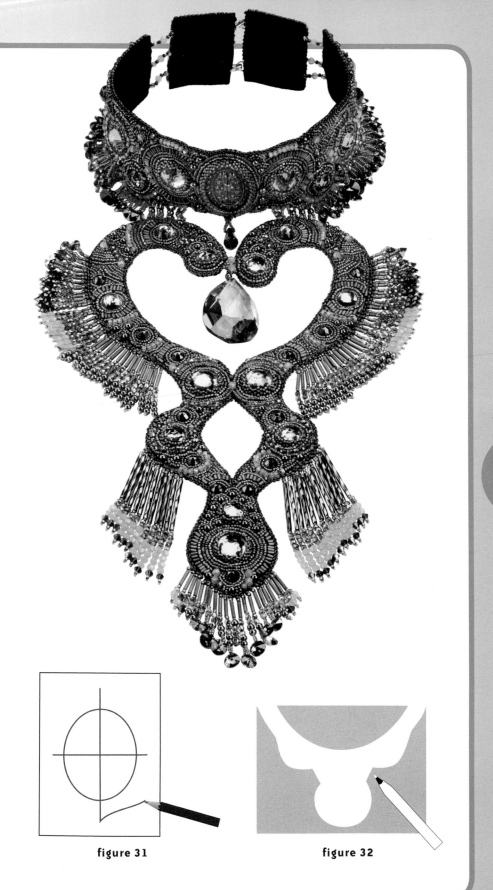

figure 31

figure 32

Design and color are personal to each one of us. I'd like to share my thoughts with you, but keep in mind that this is an area where there are no set rules. I encourage you to listen to your inner voice and use elements and colors that please you.

Color

I choose my seed beads and embellishment fun beads based on the stones or buttons that I'll be using for my focal point. Keeping it simple, I usually stick to a basic three-color system—this keeps the piece from getting too complicated or muddy. In most cases you want to enhance the focal point, not distract from it with too many colors. Occasionally, in a more monochromatic piece, I'll just use two colors of seed beads, including different sizes and finishes of the same colors.

Choose beads that enhance each other, paying attention to finishes as well as colors. Matte beads placed against shiny beads will make the shiny beads pop visually to the forefront. A palette of only shiny beads or only matte beads will look more one-dimensional.

Embellishment beads should follow suit and complement the seed beads that complement the focal point. So while you may have a great variety of beads in front of you, they should all coordinate with and complement the focal point.

If you find yourself challenged, play with a color wheel, available through art stores, for inspiration. Or take a trip to a local paint store and pick up swatches of the paint colors. You'll see how they place colors beside each other that work together.

Design

With the focal bead as a starting point, I find it easiest to work out from it when beginning my embroidery stitches. Much like a puzzle, the piece begins to take shape only after each element is put into place, without my thinking too much about what comes next. My advice on some of the projects is to let the beads take "road trips," meaning the beads will literally tell you where to go—in a nice way! For example, say you've created a bezel around your cabochon. Start embroidering out from the cabochon by backstitching a row of beads around the bezel. Next to the backstitched row place an embellishment bead, then work scallops or crosshatch around the embellishment bead. Continue in this manner, working your way out to the design lines you've drawn on your beading foundation, as opposed to jumping around the piece.

Another way to think of designing is to create beaded paths. From your focal point, begin with beads of a certain color on one side, and then continue them on the other side, bouncing the colors back and forth so the design has balance. Stitch bugle beads in one direction on the right side of a focal bead and in the opposite direction on the left side. This creates asymmetry with shape but symmetry with color. Stitch an embellishment bead, such as a 4-mm crystal, on one side of the design, then stitch the same crystal beads in a cluster of three on the other side. This creates asymmetry in design but symmetry in color, resulting in a unique and visually pleasing piece.

Tips to Use Along the Way

• Sometimes when striving for an even bead count while backstitching around a cabochon, it may appear that only one more bead will fit in the ring, resulting in an odd number. Rather than settling for the odd number, try passing your thread from the last bead into the beginning bead and giving your thread a tug. This will usually pull them together nicely and you can go on your way with even-count peyote stitch.

• If you find that your needle won't pass through a bead, don't force it. The bead may break. Simply stop and switch to a thinner needle.

• Keep your leftover beads from large projects in locking plastic bags. These bead mixes will come in handy for smaller projects like earrings and brooches.

• When stitching single-bead or picot edges, make sure your thread matches your suede. The results will be clean and professional.

• If you're using a light-colored beading foundation and the edges are too white after cutting out your beadwork, use a permanent marker to color the edges before you begin the edging.

Sherry Serafini
Untitled Cuffs, 2008
Approximately 5 x 15 cm each
Assorted beads; embroidered
PHOTO BY LARRY SANDERS

Sherry Serafini
Untitled Cuffs, 2008
Approximately 5 x 15 cm each
Assorted beads; embroidered

PHOTO BY LARRY SANDERS

Sherry Serafini
Mermaid's Attire, 2008
30.5 x 16.5 cm
Assorted beads; embroidered
PHOTO BY LARRY SANDERS

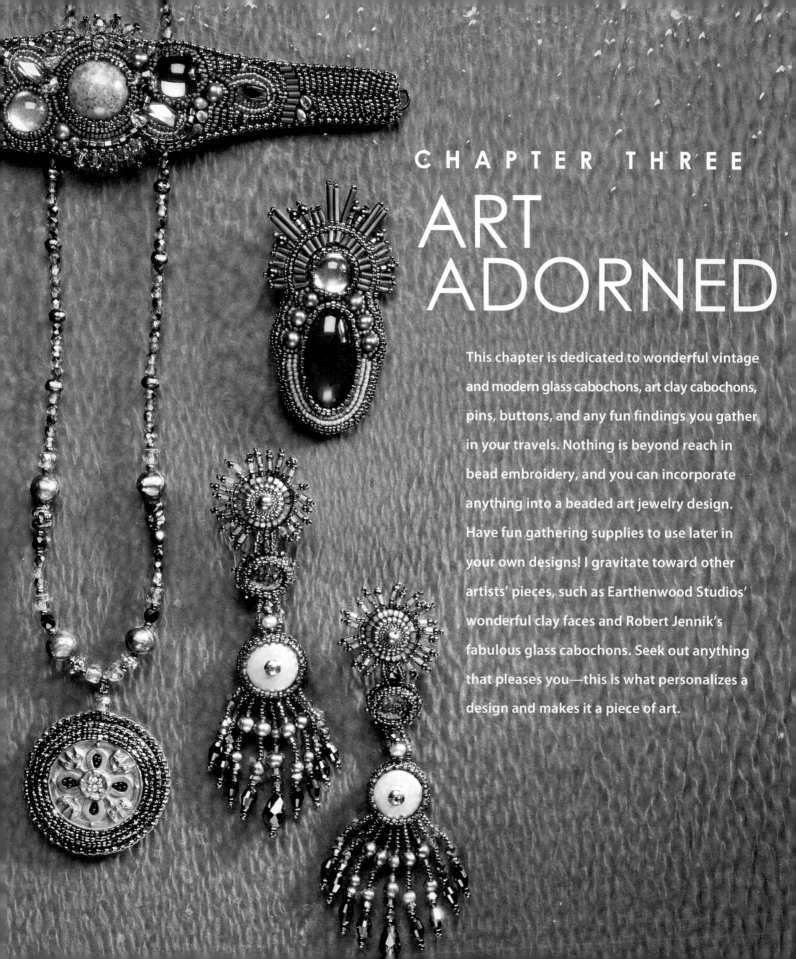

CHAPTER THREE

ART ADORNED

This chapter is dedicated to wonderful vintage and modern glass cabochons, art clay cabochons, pins, buttons, and any fun findings you gather in your travels. Nothing is beyond reach in bead embroidery, and you can incorporate anything into a beaded art jewelry design. Have fun gathering supplies to use later in your own designs! I gravitate toward other artists' pieces, such as Earthenwood Studios' wonderful clay faces and Robert Jennik's fabulous glass cabochons. Seek out anything that pleases you—this is what personalizes a design and makes it a piece of art.

SPIKED ANGEL BROOCH

The shapes of focal points often inspire my designs. In my mind, a large vintage oval cabochon topped with a smaller round one resembled a body. The way I added embellishment beads around the cabs looked like a halo—resulting in an angel. The stick fringe gives the piece pizzazz.

▶ **Design and Embroider**

1 To create a pattern, put the focal beads on a sheet of paper. To keep the space between the stones large enough to accommodate beads, leave two 15° seed bead widths between them. (I do this by placing the beads on a needle and holding them between the cabochons.) Trace around the stones and then trace a design around the stone placement. Fold the paper in half and cut out around the lines. Because you're cutting a folded piece of paper, the design will be symmetrical.

2 Trace the pattern onto the beading foundation but don't cut it out. Attach the stones with industrial strength glue or double-sided tape according to their original placement on the paper pattern.

3 Backstitch an even number of cylinder beads around the round cabochon. From the backstitched row, create a bezel by working even-count peyote stitch with cylinder beads around the cabochon. When the bezel begins to flare, work a final row with 15° As to close up the top.

4 Repeat step 3 around the oval cabochon. Use the same color cylinders and 15°s as for the bezel of the smaller cabochon to tie the piece together visually.

5 Backstitch one 4-mm pearl on each side, between the cabochons. Stitch a 3-mm bugle bead crown around the round cabochon from pearl to pearl. Backstitch the remaining pearls along both sides of the oval cabochon.

continued on next page

SUPPLIES

Basic Supplies (page 13)

Focal beads:
  1 chartreuse round cab, 12 or 14 mm
  1 dark lavender oval cab, 25 x 11 mm or similar

Size 11° metallic gold/purple iris cylinder beads, < 1 g

Size 15° seed beads:
  Color A, metallic gold, < 1 g
  Color B, blue iris matte, < 1 g
  Color C, chartreuse, < 1 g

6–8 round copper freshwater pearls, 4 mm

3-mm blue iris matte bugle beads, < 1 g

9-mm blue iris matte bugle beads, < 1 g

8–10 round gunmetal beads for fringe, 3 mm

Beading foundation, 3 x 3 inches (7.6 x 7.6 cm)

1 bar pin back, 1¼ inch (3.2 cm) long

Suede, 3 x 3 inches (7.6 x 7.6 cm)

6 Backstitch around the pearls with 15° Bs. Backstitch a couple of rows with 15° Cs around the oval cabochon from pearl to pearl. Backstitch as many rows as you like, filling in and enhancing the basic design. Backstitch a final row of 15° As around the design.

▶ Finish

1 Carefully cut the foundation flush to the beadwork. Glue the pin back to the beadwork with industrial strength adhesive. Use the tips of your scissors to make small holes in the suede to accommodate the ends of the pin back. Fit the suede over the open finding and glue it to the beadwork with white glue.

2 Stitch single-bead edging with 15°s all around the beadwork. If your thread is too short, weave through the beadwork, tie off simple knots, and begin a new thread. If it's long enough, you can weave to the top of the piece and begin the fringes.

▶ Fringe

Create simple random fringe across the top of the brooch, using a longer bugle bead in one fringe, a shorter bugle in the next fringe, and a bugle with a 3-mm bead and a seed bead for another. When finished with the fringe, weave the needle and thread through the beadwork, tying off several knots. Clip close.

32

Sherry Serafini
Dance of the Peacock, 2009
20.3 x 12.7 cm
Seed beads, crystals, vintage cabochons, feathers; embroidered

SUPPLIES

Basic Supplies (page 13)

Focal beads:
2 gold-tone synthetic
or real shell beads,
approximately 16–18 mm

Size 11° metallic
olive green cylinder beads, < 1 g

Size 15° metallic
gold seed beads, < 1 g

12–20 crystal AB bugle beads, 5 mm

20–30 gold-tone
freshwater pearls, 3 mm

6–8 round pale green beads, 4 mm

6–10 keshi pearls

2 crystal sequins, 5 mm

8 gold-tone freshwater stick pearls

2 pieces of beading foundation,
each 2 x 2 inches (5.1 x 5.1 cm)

2 earring posts

2 pieces of suede,
each 2 x 2 inches (5.1 x 5.1 cm)

SHELLZ EARRINGS

Because of their irregular shapes, shells are a fun beading challenge.
Whether you're using real shells or fakes, make sure your peyote
stitch bezel is tight around them. I was enticed by acrylic shells sold
on a strand. They have holes in them, but the peyote bezel hides
them. Stick pearls create a textured fringe for these earrings.

▶ Design and Embroider

1 Using industrial strength adhesive or double-sided tape, attach the shells to the centers of the foundation pieces. Backstitch around one of the shells with cylinder beads, trying to keep an even number, though you may end up with an odd number. With irregular-shaped focal points like shells, it isn't as important to get an even number.

2 From your backstitched row, continue with cylinder beads and work odd- or even-count peyote stitch around the shell until the beads start to flare out slightly. Stitch a final row with 15°s to close up the top of the bezel.

3 Stitching out from the bezel, backstitch 6 to 10 bugle beads in place above the shell. My shells accommodated 6 bugle beads.

4 Backstitch a row of 3-mm freshwater pearls below the bugle beads, along one side of the bezel. My shells allowed for 12 pearls. Next, backstitch three 4-mm round beads.

5 For the remaining space around the bezel, stitch the keshi pearls in place using the stop stitch method and 15°s. Turning the stop stitch into a top stitch, stitch a crystal sequin in place on top of the bugle beads, using a 15°. Carefully cut the excess foundation flush against the beadwork.

▶ Finish

1 Glue a post to the back of the beadwork with industrial-strength adhesive and allow it to dry. Cut a small slit in the suede, position it over the post, and use white glue to attach it to the back of the beadwork and the post. Cut the suede flush against the beadwork.

2 With 15°s, work a single-bead edging around the earring.

▶ Embellish

1 Rethread your needle with a single strand of thread, tie a knot, and clip the knot so it's small enough to anchor in the existing beadwork. Anchor the knot underneath some of the larger beads toward the bottom of the earring component. Pass the needle through one of the cylinder beads in the rows of your peyote stitch.

2 Pick up two 15°s, 1 stick pearl, and 2 more 15°s. Pass the needle through the next cylinder bead in the same row (figure 1). Repeat twice more.

3 Weave the needle toward the bottom of the beadwork to find the two bottom center edge beads. Exit one of the edge beads and pick up three 15°s, one 4-mm bead, six 15°s, 1 stick pearl, and six 15°s.

4 Pass back through the 4-mm bead. Pick up three 15°s and pass through the edge bead beside the one first exited (figure 2). Weave through the beadwork and tie off several small knots. Clip close.

Repeat all the steps to make a second earring, but mirror the orientation and placement of the beads.

figure 1

figure 2

34

SWEET SIMPLICITY NECKLACE

Sometimes a focal bead is so beautiful and strong that it doesn't need heavy bead embroidery around it—it simply speaks for itself. Case in point: the metal clay piece by Kelly Russell that's the centerpiece of this necklace. You can use any focal point with a flat back.

SUPPLIES

Basic Supplies (page 13)

Focal bead:
    20–30 mm flat-backed
    round stone or art bead

Size 15° seed beads:
    Color A, dark bronze, 2–3 g
    Color B, black, < 1 g

**Size 11° gold metallic
seed beads, 2–3 g**

1 pale rose Czech bead, 4 mm

**Assorted 3-mm round, 8-mm
metallic, and 3-mm rondelle fun
beads for necklace strand**

**Beading foundation, 3 x 3 inches
(7.6 x 7.6 cm)**

Suede, 3 x 3 inches (7.6 x 7.6 cm)

▶ Design and Embroider

1 Glue the focal bead to the center of the foundation with industrial strength adhesive and allow it to dry.

2 Thread a needle with 1 yard (91.4 cm) of thread and tie a simple knot. Pass the needle up beside the focal bead. With 15° As, backstitch around the focal bead. Backstitch 2 more rows of 15° As around the first one.

3 If your focal point is like the one I chose, there are tiny cutouts in the piece. I chose to stitch 15° Bs in those cutouts to add dimension.

4 Weave the needle and thread through the bead-work, tie off several knots, and clip the thread close. Carefully cut the excess foundation flush against your beadwork. Using 15° Bs, stitch a single-bead edging around the design. Knot the thread on the back of the beadwork and clip close.

▶ Finish the Pendant

Attach the suede to the back of the beadwork with white glue. When the glue is dry, trim the suede close to the beadwork. Rethread your needle with 18 inches (45.7 cm) of thread and tie a simple knot. Bury the knot under the beadwork and exit on the edge of the beadwork. Stitch a second single-bead edging with 11°s around the beadwork, connecting your last bead to your first bead.

▶ Make the Bail

You can hang this simple pendant from anything you wish. A simple sterling neckband, a strand of beads that match the beads used in the embroidering—the choice is yours. Have some fun!

Pass through one of the edge beads. Pick up the 4-mm Czech bead, one 11°, and enough 15°s to create a loop big enough to go around your chosen necklace strand. Pass back through the 11°, the Czech bead, and the edge bead you began with. Repeat the thread path several times for strength. Weave the needle and thread down through the beadwork, tie off several small knots, and clip close.

BEE BRACELET

I love the effect of gluing a clear acrylic bubble over an image on paper. Rubber stamp and craft stores offer a variety of playthings for beaders, including flat-backed domes with which you can create instant cabochons using clip art or other images. I paired a bee cabochon with art glass cabochons by Robert Jennik for a very original piece.

SUPPLIES

Basic Supplies (page 13)

Focal beads:
- 1 clear domed bubble, 18–30 mm
- 1 black and white bee image or image of your choice*
- 2 cabochons, 18 mm

Size 11° cylinder beads:
- Color A, green/gold luster, 3 g
- Color B, matte black, 3 g

Size 15° metallic gold seed beads, 1 g

Size 11° metallic gold seed beads, 5 g

64–70 faux pearls, 2 mm

65–75 crystal bicone beads, 4 mm

70–80 crystal bicone beads, 3 mm— same color as 4-mm bicones

Diamond Glaze dimensional adhesive glaze

Small paintbrush

Beading foundation:
- 1 piece 3 x 3 inches (7.6 x 7.6 cm)
- 2 pieces 2 x 2 inches (5.1 x 5.1 cm)

Suede:
- 1 piece 3 x 3 inches (7.6 x 7.6 cm)
- 2 pieces 2 x 2 inches (5.1 x 5.1 cm)

3-loop clasp, 1 inch (2.5 cm) wide

* If you're using a photocopy, make sure it's from a laser printer, not an inkjet, and use high-quality paper. **Note:** Before using an artist's imagery, please check on copyright laws.

▶ Components

1 To glue the paper image to the back of the acrylic dome, use the paintbrush to spread a thin layer of dimensional adhesive glaze over the front of the entire image. Press the glued surface onto the flat side of the glass gem, working out any air bubbles with your fingers. Allow the adhesive to dry, then apply a thin layer to the back of the paper to further protect the image.

2 Attach the dome and cabochons to the pieces of beading foundation with industrial strength glue or double-sided tape; if you use glue, allow it to dry.

3 Backstitch an even number of color A cylinder beads around the dome. Using the same cylinder beads, work several rows of peyote stitch off the backstitched beads to create a bezel. When the bezel begins to flare out, work a final peyote stitch row with 15°s to close up around the dome.

4 Carefully cut the excess foundation flush against the beadwork, glue to the piece of suede with white glue, and allow to dry. Carefully trim the suede flush to the foundation.

5 Work single-bead edging around this component with 11° seed beads. Set aside.

6 Backstitch an even number of color B cylinder beads around each of the cabochons. Using the same cylinder beads, work several rows of peyote stitch off the backstitched beads to create bezels. When the bezels begin to flare out, work final peyote stitch rows with 15°s to close up around the cabochons.

7 Backstitch the 2-mm pearls around the bezeled cabochons.

8 Carefully cut the excess foundation flush against the beadwork, glue the beadwork to the piece of suede with white glue, and allow it to dry. Carefully trim the suede flush to the foundation.

9 Work single-bead edging around these components with 11° seed beads.

▶ Assemble

1 Thread your needle with 3 feet (44.1 cm) of thread, double it, and tie a knot. Locate the 3 centered beads on the side of the dome component. Bury the knot and weave through the beadwork to exit one of the edge beads on either side of the center bead. Pick up one 11°, one 4-mm crystal, one 11°, and pass through an edge bead on one of the cabochon components to attach.

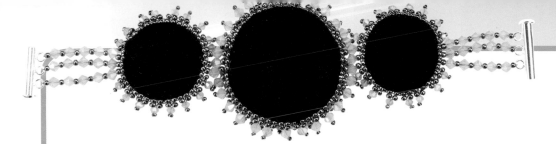

2 Weave through the beading foundation and pass through the next edge bead. Pick up one 11°, one 4-mm crystal, one 11°, and pass through the center edge bead on the domed component. Create a third connection the same way. Tie off in the beadwork (figure 1).

3 Connect the second cabochon component to the opposite side of the domed component.

4 The band is formed the same way as the connectors. Locate the 3 edge beads on the opposite side of the smaller components, parallel to the connectors. Cut 4 feet (121.9 cm) of thread, double it, and tie a knot at the end. Bury the thread in the beadwork of one of your smaller components and pass through one of the edge beads on either side of the center one. String on one 11° and one 4-mm crystal; repeat this pattern for the length that you need for your wrist, allowing 1 inch (2.5 cm) for the clasp. String one 11°, pass through a loop on the clasp and pass back through all of the beads in the strand once more.

5 Repeat this pattern through the center edge bead, picking up the middle loop of the clasp, and once again for the final strand and loop. Repeat the pattern once more through the edge bead on the other side of the center, picking up the third loop of the clasp (figure 2).

6 Tie off the thread in the beadwork, hide the knot, and repeat the process on the other side of the bracelet.

▶ **Embellish**

1 Thread a needle with 4 feet (1.2 m) of thread, double it, and tie a knot. Weave through the beadwork on the dome component and exit an edge bead beside one of the connectors. Pick up one 11°, one 4-mm crystal, and one 15°. Skip over the 15° and pass back through the crystal. Pick up one 11° and pass down through the edge bead beside the one you previously exited. Repeat around the edge until you reach the connectors on the opposite side. If you have only one edge bead remaining at the end, exit this bead, pick up

one 11°, one 4-mm crystal, and one 15°, pass over the 15°, through the crystal and the 11°, and into the same edge bead. Weave the thread to the other side of the dome component and stitch the other side in the same manner.

2 Embellish the smaller components the same way, but use 3-mm crystals in place of the 4-mm crystals.

3 Thread a thinner needle with doubled thread or use braided beading thread. Pass the needle and thread up through the beading foundation of the center dome component and up through the bezel wall to exit a cylinder bead in the second or third row. Pick up one 15°, one 3-mm crystal, and one 15°. Skip over the 15° and pass back through the crystal. Pick up one 15° and pass through the next cylinder bead in the row (figure 3). Continue around in this manner until you reach the starting point. Weave the thread through the bezel beads and tie off several knots. Clip the thread close.

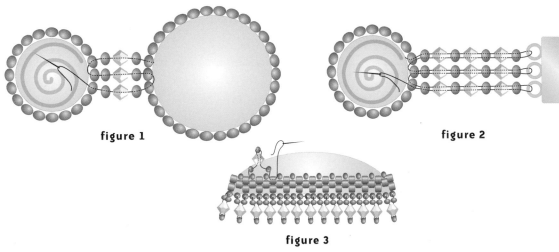

figure 1

figure 2

figure 3

RAYS OF SUNSHINE
FREEFORM CUFF

The challenge of working with brighter colors drew me to the cabochons in this cuff. The happy orange color of the largest cabochon dictated the color choices of the beads and cabs stitched around it, and the combinations create a vibrant collage.

Working with colors you normally don't choose is a good way to challenge yourself and get outside the box.

► Set the Cabochons

1 Draw a line down the vertical and horizontal centers of a sheet of paper to help determine where your cabochons will be placed. Position the cabochons where you want them and trace around them on the paper. Set the cabochons aside.

2 Fold the paper in half and cut a shape that pleases you. You can draw the shape first or cut freeform. Play until you have a shape that you like. Cut the paper pattern to your wrist size, deducting 1½ inches (3.8 cm) for the clasp. Trace the pattern onto beading foundation.

3 Glue the cabochons to the foundation with industrial adhesive, following the placement indicated from your pattern. Allow the glue to dry.

4 Backstitch around the largest cabochon with 15° As. From the backstitched row, use the same beads to work peyote stitch up the sides of the cabochon, creating a bezel. For the last row, close up with 15° Bs.

5 Repeat step 4 for the other cabochons, using different colors of 15°s; if you used a matte 15° to do the main bezel, switch to a shiny one for the closing-up row. This will really enhance your design.

► Embroider

1 Now let your imagination take over. Begin embroidering the rest of the cuff with fun beads. Following the shape of the cabochons, work out from them using backstitch and stop stitches. Experiment with texture as you backstitch, placing matte beads beside shiny ones; this allows the colors to pop. If you're not the type to just go with the flow, try drawing your design directly onto the foundation with a permanent marker. This is your time to have fun—listen to your inner voice, follow your heart, and bead!

2 Keep the ends of the cuff simple by stitching with crosshatch stitch for about the last inch (2.5 cm) of each end.

3 After you've embroidered the entire cuff and are satisfied with the results, make sure the beads are secure and the stitches aren't loose. Stitch crystal sequins with stop stitch randomly throughout the beadwork, to add sparkle. Make sure to stitch through the crystals at least twice.

► Finish

1 Carefully cut off the excess foundation flush against the beadwork, being careful not to snip any threads.

continued on next page

SUPPLIES

Basic Supplies (page 13)

Focal beads:

> 1 orange cabochon, 20 mm

> 1 green cabochon, 18 mm

> 1 yellowish-red cabochon, 16 mm

Size 15° seed beads:

> Color A, rainbow bronze, 2–3 g

> Color B, metallic blue iris, 2–3 g

> Color C, matte green, 2–3 g

Assorted freshwater pearls, oblong crystals, etc., to use as fun beads

6–8 green crystal sequins, 5 mm

Size 11° metallic bronze seed beads, 3 g

10 orange round or bicone crystals for fringes, 4 mm

3-mm matte brown bugle beads, 3 g

Hook-and-eye clasp

Beading foundation, 3 x 7 inches (7.6 x 17.8 cm)

Suede, 3 x 7 inches (7.6 x 17.8 cm)

41

2 Thread a needle with 24 inches (61 cm) of thread, double it, and tie a knot at the end. Anchor the thread in the foundation at one end of the cuff. Sew the hook part of the clasp to the end of the cuff so that the hook faces away from the beaded surface. Sew the loop to the other end, making sure there's enough of the loop sticking out from the edge for the hook attachment to go through.

3 Use a toothpick to roll a thin, even layer of white glue onto the backside of the beaded piece. Stay ⅛ inch (3 mm) away from the edges of the beadwork so the needle and thread will glide easily through both layers in the final steps. Place the glued beadwork down against the suede. Allow the glue to dry, and then carefully cut the excess suede flush against the beadwork.

4 Stitch single-bead edging with 11°s all the way around the beadwork. Weave through the beadwork, tie off simple knots, and clip the threads.

▶ Embellishment Fringe

1 Thread your needle with a double thread and tie a knot. Bury the knot in the beadwork and exit an edge bead where the large center cabochon starts its curve. Pick up one 15°, 1 crystal, and one 15°.

2 Skip over the last 15° strung, pass through the crystal then down through the same edge bead you initially exited, to anchor the first fringe.

3 Pass the needle and thread up through the next edge bead and repeat this process, following the curve of the cabochon.

4 Weave through to the other side of the cabochon by traveling with your needle and thread underneath the beadwork, or knot off and begin a new thread on the other side to make more fringes.

Sherry Serafini
Rocks, 2009
33 x 15.2 x 2.5 cm
Seed beads, crystals; right angle weave, embroidered
PHOTO BY LARRY SANDERS

42

FUNKY EARRINGS

Find a bunch of colorful beads of different sizes and shapes, use them to create small components, and fit them together like a puzzle. Add some fringe and an ear wire or post, and *voilà*—you've got a fun and fabulous pair of earrings.

SUPPLIES

Basic Supplies (page 13)

Focal beads:
    2 pale lavender round, flat disc beads, 12 mm
    2 topaz oval cabochons, 10 mm
    2 antiqued brass round spacer beads, 10 mm

Freshwater pearls, 3–4 mm:
    12–14 color A, lavender
    10–12 color B, gold

Size 11° green/gold luster cylinder beads, < 1 g

Size 15° seed beads:
    Color A, dark lavender, < 1 g
    Color B, dark metallic gold, 1 g
    Color C, copper luster, < 1 g

2 blue iris rondelles, 2 mm

2-mm crystal bicones:
    12 color A, purple
    30 color B, teal AB

Size 11° lavender hex beads, < 1 g

Size 11° dark metallic gold seed beads, < 1 g

2 purple drop crystal beads, 8 mm

16 dark blue AB barrel crystal beads, 4 mm

6 pieces of beading foundation, each 1½ x 1½ inches (3.8 x 3.8 cm)

2 ear posts

6 pieces of suede, each 1½ x 1½ inches (3.8 x 3.8 cm)

Glue the 6 focal beads to the centers of the foundation pieces with industrial-strength glue and allow them to dry. When gluing the spacers, be careful to keep the glue away from the center hole; you'll need to stitch through this hole later. Make both earrings at the same time to keep them symmetrical.

▶ Top Components

1 Stitch a 3-mm A-colored pearl to the center of both spacer beads. Backstitch a row of cylinder beads around the spacers.

2 Carefully cut the excess foundation flush against the beadwork. Glue the ear posts to the back of the components, and allow them to dry. Cut a small slit on two suede pieces so that they can slide over the posts on the backs of the top components. Glue the suede to the back of the beadwork with white glue and allow it to dry.

3 Cut the excess suede flush against the beadwork. Using 15° As, stitch a single-bead edging around the component and set aside.

▶ Middle Components

1 Backstitch an even number of 15° Bs around the oval cabochons. Using 15° Bs, work even-count peyote stitch from the backstitched rows, creating bezels around the cabochons. The height of your particular cabochon will determine the number of rows to stitch around and up the stone.

2 Cut the excess foundation flush against the beadwork, glue suede to the back of the pieces with white glue, and allow them to dry.

3 Cut the excess suede flush with the beadwork and stitch a single-bead edging with size 15° As around the component. Set aside.

▶ Bottom Components

1 Using the stop stitch method, set a rondelle over the center hole of each disk with 15° As as your stop bead.

2 Backstitch an even number of 15° Bs around the disks. Using 15° Bs, work even-count peyote stitch from the backstitched rows, creating bezels around the disks. With 15° Cs, stitch a final taut row to close up the bezels. This second color adds some dazzle.

3 Carefully cut the excess foundation flush against the beadwork and glue it to the suede with white glue. Allow this to dry and cut the excess suede flush against the beadwork.

4 Stitch a single-bead edging with 15° As around the component.

▶ Assemble

1 Single thread a size-13 needle with two feet (61 cm) of thread and tie a knot at the end. Clip the ends neatly so they don't show. Bury the knot between the beads on the top component and weave through to exit an edge bead.

2 Pick up two 15° Bs, 1 crystal B, and two 15° Bs. Locate the center edge bead on one of the lengthwise walls on the middle component. Pass the needle and thread through this center edge bead to connect the two pieces.

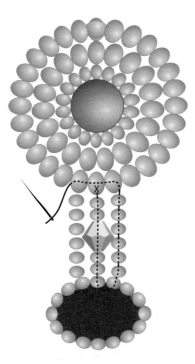

figure 1

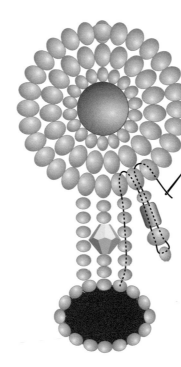

figure 2

figure 3

3 Pass the needle up through the edge bead directly beside the one you came down through. Pick up six 15° Bs and pass through the edge bead directly beside the one you originally exited on the top component. Weave through the foundation and exit the edge bead on the opposite side of the one you began with (figure 1). Pick up six 15° Bs and pass through the corresponding bead on the middle component. Pass through all three connectors again to strengthen.

4 Weave down through one of the connectors to the middle component. Pick up one 15° B, 1 hex bead, one 11°, and one 15° B. Skip over the last 15° and pass back through all the beads and into the edge bead you started with, creating a simple fringe (figure 2). Exit the next edge bead and repeat to add fringe around the top component to the other side of

the connectors, alternating one or two 11°s below the hex bead. Weave through some of the cylinder beads backstitched around the spacers and tie off several small knots to secure. Clip close.

5 Locate the center bottom of the oval middle component and pass through the edge bead opposite the center connector at the top. Pick up one 11°, 1 crystal B, one 11°, 1 pearl B, and one 11°. Pass through an edge bead on the bottom component.

6 Pass up through the next edge bead. Pick up three 15° Bs, 1 crystal A, three 15° Bs, and pass through the edge bead next to the connector on the middle component. Repeat on the other side and go through all the connectors again to strengthen (figure 3).

7 Pass up through the edge bead beside a connector on the middle component and pick up one 15° A. Pass down through

the next edge bead. Bring the needle up through the edge bead beside the one you just exited and pick up one 15° A. Repeat around the entire component. Weave the thread through the beadwork and tie off the knots to secure.

▶ **Fringe**

1 Adding fringe is always fun. Using the double-needle method (page 22) with 24 inches (61 cm) of thread, string one 15° B for the stop bead and slide it to the center of the thread. Onto both needles pick up one 11°, 1 crystal drop, one 11°, 1 crystal B, one 11°, 1 hex bead, 1 pearl A, 1 hex bead, one 15° C, 1 pearl B, one 15° C, and six 15° As. Pass one of the needles up through the center edge bead on the bottom component, then pass the other needle through the same center edge bead.

continued on next page

2 Pass 1 needle down through an edge bead beside the one just exited, and pass the other needle down through the one on the opposite side. Onto each needle, pick up five 15°B, one 15° C, 1 pearl A, one 15° C, five 15° B, 1 pearl B, 1 crystal B, one 11°, 1 barrel bead, one 11°, and one 15° B. Skip over the 15° and pass each needle up through all the beads in the row and through the edge bead first exited. Pass down through the edge bead beside this fringe row.

3 Continuing with both needles, add 3 more fringes to each side in these patterns:

• Four 15° Bs, one 15° C, 1 pearl A, one 15° C, four 15° Bs, 1 pearl B, 1 crystal B, one 11°, 1 barrel bead, one 11°, one 15° A (stop bead).

• Four 15° Bs, one 15° C, 1 crystal A, one 15° C, four 15° Bs, 2 crystal Bs, one 11°, 1 barrel bead, one 11°, one 15° A (stop bead).

• Same as the previous row, with three 15° Bs in place of four 15° Bs.

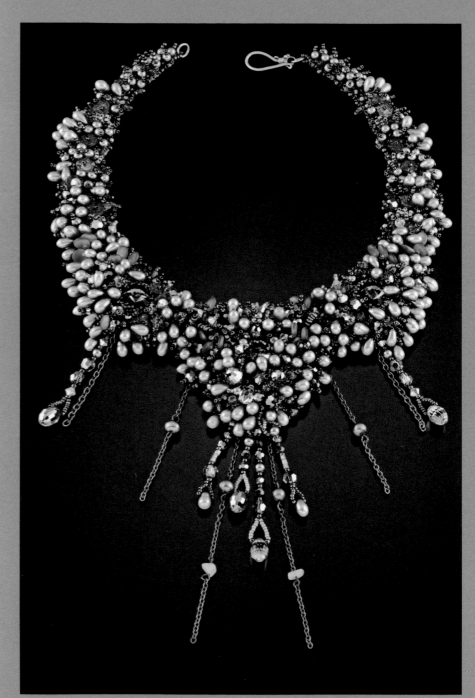

Sherry Serafini
Pearle Jam, 2007
20.3 x 12.7 x 0.6 cm
Pearls, crystals, seed beads, chains; embroidered
PHOTO BY LARRY SANDERS

GODDESS PENDANT

I love using beads with faces on them in my bead embroidery, and this lovely focal bead, created by Earthenwood Studios, is perfect for my goddess. Just as we're all unique in our looks and personalities, your beadwork will be unique when created around one-of-a-kind components. This pendant is symmetrical in shape, but asymmetrical within the beadwork, as the embroidered beads take little road trips around the face. The instructions tell you to use beads of your choosing; these may include vintage nailheads, bugles, crystals, pearls—anything goes!

SUPPLIES

Basic Supplies (page 13)

Focal bead:
   Blue face cabochon,
   15 x 23 mm

Size 15° seed beads:
   Color A, matte green
   purple iris, < 1 g
   Color B, sea foam lined
   crystal AB, < 1 g
   Color C, black, < 1 g

**Fun beads of your choice
in coordinating colors**

Silver neck ring

**Beading foundation,
5 x 5 inches (12.7 x 12.7 cm)**

**Poster board, 5 x 5 inches
(12.7 x 12.7 cm)**

**Suede, 5 x 5 inches
(12.7 x 12.7 cm)**

▶ **Design and Embroider**

1 Place your focal bead on a sheet of paper and play with designs for your pendant until you're happy with what you see. Use the fold in half method to cut out the design if you'd like it to be symmetrical. (You can also go for a totally asymmetrical design.) Trace this template onto the beading foundation. Glue the cabochon into place with industrial strength glue and allow to dry. If you desire, use a permanent marker to draw some designs onto the foundation.

2 After the glue has dried, backstitch an even number of 15° A beads around the face cabochon. From the backstitched row, work even-count peyote stitch with 15° As to form a bezel around the cabochon. Work peyote stitch up the sides of the cabochon and secure it with a taut final row of 15° As.

3 When the peyote bezel has been completed, begin to design with bead embroidery. Using a fine point black pen, draw lines on the foundation to indicate where you'd like your beaded paths. Stitch rows of crosshatching with 15°Bs, and fill in with fun beads using backstitch and stop stitch. If you change your mind in the middle of beading, just backstitch beads over the drawn lines—no long-term commitments here! **Tip:** Placing shiny beads beside matte ones will make the colors pop.

▶ **Finish**

1 After you've bead embroidered your pendant and are pleased with the design, carefully cut the excess foundation flush against the beadwork. If your pendant is on the large side, lay the beadwork onto a piece of poster board. Trace around the beadwork onto the poster board. Cut the poster board out about $\frac{1}{16}$ inch (1.6 mm) smaller than the beadwork so you'll be able to get your needle and thread through the edges in the final phase. Glue the beadwork to the poster board with white glue.

2 Use white glue to attach the beadwork with the poster board backing to the suede and allow to dry. Cut the excess suede from the pendant flush against the beadwork.

3 Work single-bead edging with 15° C beads.

4 Locate the center 3 beads at the top of the pendant and create a simple loop bail with 15° Cs to fit over your chosen neck ring or strand of beads. Add fringe by working through the edge beads at the bottom with fun beads.

Sherry Serafini

Road Warrior, 2009

61 x 17.8 x 2.5 cm

Seed beads, nail heads, bugle beads,
license plates, metal, cabochons by
Gary Wilson; embroidered

PHOTO BY LARRY SANDERS

CLASSY LADY NECKPIECE

Make a design more interesting by mixing things up. I chose a beautiful ivory-colored goddess and paired her up with a funky art glass cabochon by Robert Jennik. To pull two diverse focal beads together, select cabachons of the same width and use the same colors to enhance them. The interesting part begins when you randomly stitch beaded paths around the focal points, creating one flowing, cohesive design.

▶ Design and Embroider

1 Make a paper pattern, drawing a circular shape with horizontal and vertical lines to accommodate your neck size. Using this as your guide, determine the shape of your neckpiece by laying your focal beads down on the lines, keeping them ¼ inch (6 mm) apart to accommodate the beads that will be backstitched around them. Trace around the stones and play with several design options. Draw your chosen design, fold the paper in half, and cut out the pattern. For the two side units, simply cut the pattern off 1 inch (2.5 cm) away from the largest part of the top cabochon. You can use the template provided below instead.

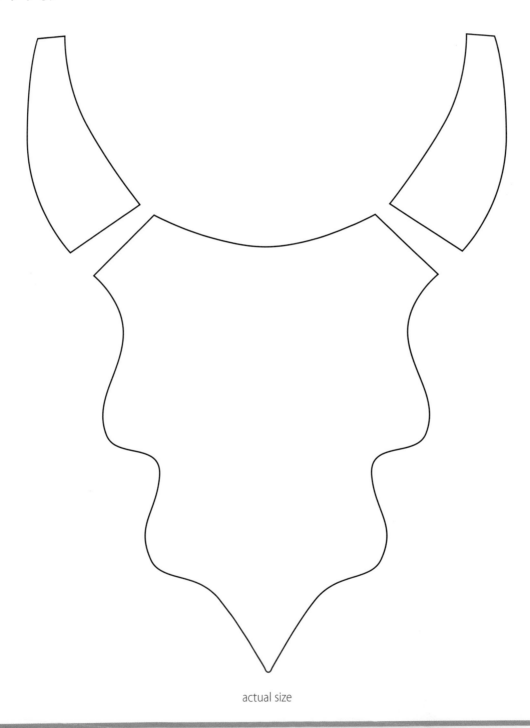

actual size

2 Trace the patterns onto the foundation. Glue the focal stones onto them with industrial adhesive and allow them to dry.

3 Backstitch an even number of cylinder beads around the oval cabochon. From the backstitched row, peyote stitch several rows with cylinder beads to form a bezel around the cabochon. When the bezel begins to flare, peyote stitch a final row with 15° As to close the top of the bezel.

4 Repeat step 3, with the same beads, around the round cabochon. Beading around both focal beads in the same colors visually pulls them together.

5 Backstitch around both cabochons with two rows of 15° Bs. Where the cabochons meet at the center point, backstitch a 6-mm nail head on each side. Backstitch seed pearls between the nail heads and the two cabochons to fill in these areas (figure 1). I call this "painting with your beads."

continued on next page

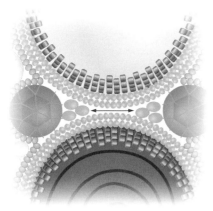

figure 1

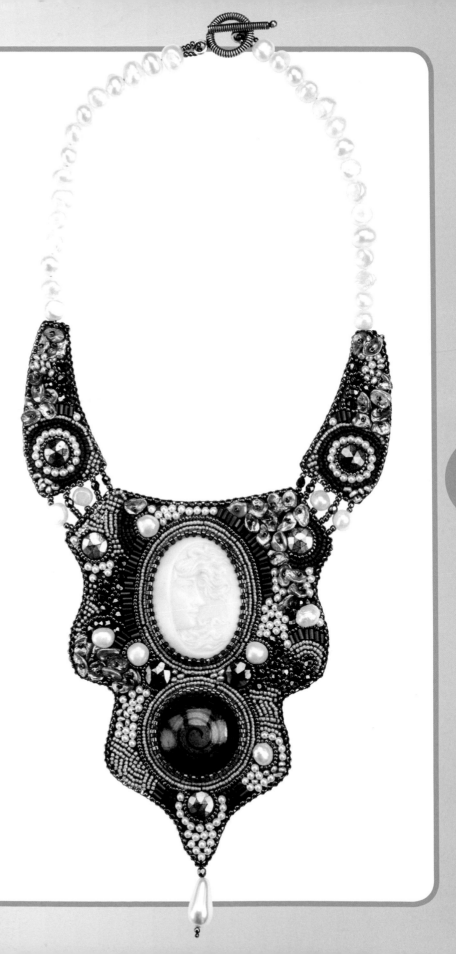

53

6 Backstitch a nail head centered below the smaller cabochon. Now backstitch with 15° Cs around the entire design to tie it together. Backstitch 2 freshwater pearls in the corners between the cabochons, just above the nail heads. Backstitch a row of 15° Cs around the pearls.

7 Now you can have some designing fun. Using the pattern as your guide, bead embroider across the design, creating varied beaded paths and clusters. Use stop stitch with 15° Cs and keshi pearls, and backstitch with round pearls and bugles. Asymmetry can appear very symmetrical if you use the same colors on both sides of the piece. For example, a cluster of pearls on a right-hand corner can be visually echoed on the other side of the design by stitching another cluster in a higher area on the left. If it helps, draw guidelines where you'd like your beaded paths to appear. With a larger piece like this one, cross-hatched rows of beads are a lovely way to fill in around certain areas, so experiment and play with this technique.

▶ Finish

1 When you've completed the bead embroidery, cut the excess foundation flush against the beadwork. Trace around the piece onto poster board to create a stable backing between the beadwork and the suede. Cut the poster board slightly smaller than the beadwork to allow the needle to pass through the edges for finishing. Glue the poster board to the back of the beadwork with white glue and allow it to dry. Glue the suede to the back of the poster board with white glue. When it's dry, cut the suede flush against the beadwork.

2 Use 11's to work single-bead edging around the entire design. Set it aside.

▶ Side Units

1 The asymmetrical center will be the main focus, with two symmetrical side units enhancing it. Bead embroider the two side units as mirror images of each other. To better control the process, I often work both pieces at the same time to ensure that I'm doing the same stitches on both. Because these pieces aren't large, a poster board backing isn't necessary. When the embroidery is complete, glue suede to the back of the beadwork panels and work single-bead edging around them with the 11's.

2 To connect all 3 pieces, lay them out with the 2 side units at the top edges of the central piece. Double-thread a needle and weave through the beadwork to exit an edge bead at the top of one side of the central piece. Pick up one 11°, 1 fire-polished bead, and one 11°. Pass through

the corresponding edge bead on the side unit to connect the 2 pieces together (figure 2). Skip over the edge bead directly beside the one entered, and exit through the next edge bead. You will be skipping over an edge bead for all the connections, for proper spacing.

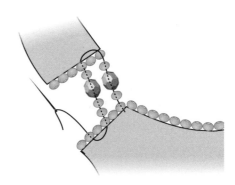

figure 2

3 As you work the connector strands down the sides, you will need to add extra beads to accommodate the widening spaces between the central piece and the two sides. For the second connection pick up one 11°, 1 fire-polished bead, and two 11°s. Pass through the corresponding edge bead on the central piece. The next connector will be one 11°, 1 freshwater pearl, and one 11°. The next connector will be three 11°s, 1 fire-polished bead, and two 11°s. The final connector will be two 11°s, 1 freshwater pearl, and two 11°s. Weave through the beadwork, tie off several small knots, and clip close. **Note:** Your connections may vary in count, depending on how many edge beads you are working with on your particular design.

4 Repeat steps 1 and 2 exactly, to connect the second side unit. Feel free to use different beads in your connectors! Play with the design until you like what you see.

▶ Necklace Strands

Single thread your needle and tie a knot at the end. Weave through one side unit to exit the edge bead at the top and center. Pick up as many freshwater pearls as you would like for the length of your necklace. Pick up four 11°s, half of the clasp, and four 11°s. Pass back through the entire row of pearls and back through the edge bead you began with. Weave through the beadwork, tie off several small knots, and clip close. Repeat on the other side.

▶ Finish

Weave through the bottom of the beadwork to exit the edge bead at the center bottom. Add one 11°, 1 fire-polished bead, the drop, and two 11°s to the bottom of the neckpiece (figure 3).

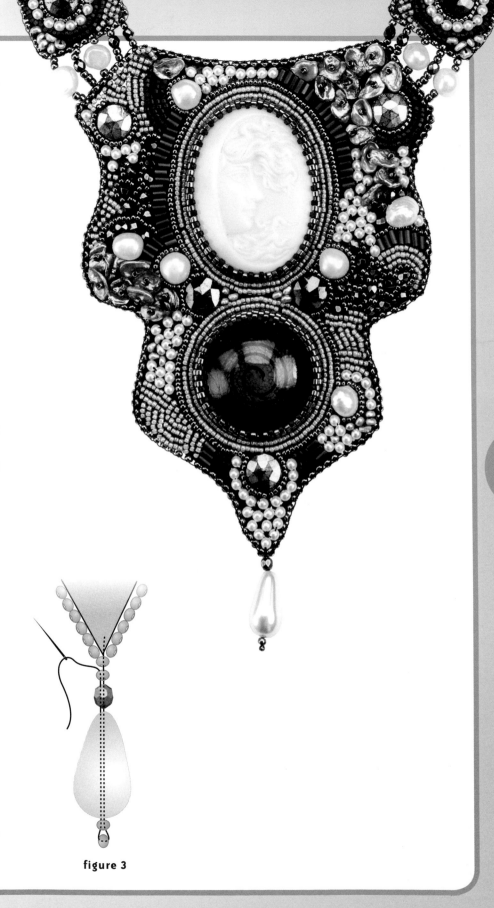

figure 3

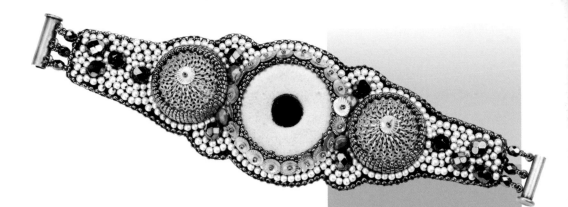

DONUT & PEARL CUFF

The surprising combination of a big, bold donut with small and subtle pearls creates a cuff that's elegant and edgy at the same time. Domed filigree buttons and gear-like sequins give the piece a hint of steampunk style.

▶ Set the Focal Beads

1 Draw lines down the vertical and horizontal center of a sheet of paper, with each line representing the central axis of the cuff. Place the donut at the intersection of the lines and trace around it. Place the 2 buttons on either side of the drawn donut shape, leaving space between them for bezels and embroidery, and trace around those. Draw 2 more lines along the length of the pattern, far enough away from the donut shape to allow for a bezel and embroidery. This simply gives you guidelines for the width of the cuff (figure 1).

2 Cut the paper pattern out on these lines. Determine your wrist size, leaving space for your chosen clasp and connectors, and

cut the ends to that length. Trace the pattern onto your beading foundation. Glue the donuts and buttons to the foundation with industrial-strength glue, following the placement indicated from your pattern, and allow them to dry.

3 Backstitch an even number of cylinder beads around the donut. From the backstitched row, peyote stitch a few rows up the sides of the donut, creating a bezel. When the bezel begins to flare, peyote stitch a final row with 15°s to close up the bezel.

4 Repeat step 3, to create bezels around the buttons, using the same cylinder beads and 15°s.

continued on next page

continued on next page

SUPPLIES

Basic Supplies (page 13)

Focal beads:

- 1 celadon donut-shaped, flat-back stone, 30–40 mm
- 2 gold metal high-domed buttons or beads with holes on top and shanks cut off the backs, 20–25 mm

Size 11° metallic gold cylinder beads, 4–5 g

Size 15° metallic gold seed beads, 4–5 g

144 faux or real white round pearls, 2 mm

12–20 purple AB Czech beads, 6 mm

22–28 iridescent sequins, 6 mm

22–28 clear AB sequins, 3mm

4 purple vintage nail heads, 4 mm

Size 11° metallic dark-gold seed beads, 5 g

6 purple AB Czech beads, 4 mm

Beading foundation, 3 x 7 inches (7.6 x 17.8 cm)

1 brass bar clasp with 3–4 loops, ¾ inch (1.9 cm)

Suede, 3 x 7 inches (7.6 x 17.8 cm)

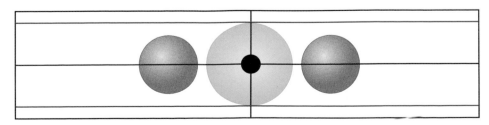

figure 1

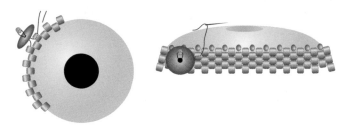

figure 2

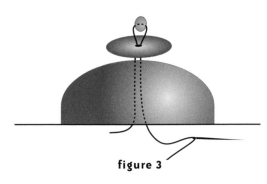

figure 3

▶ Embroider

1 Using pearls, backstitch around the donut and then the buttons. Stitch one 6-mm Czech bead at each of the 4 corners of the donut, between the donut and the buttons. Backstitch another row of pearls around the donut and around the Czech beads. At this point you have the option of making the cuff wider (if you left enough width on the foundation) by adding as many rows of pearls as you want. I kept mine simple with just a couple of rows.

2 Using pearls, embroider along the length of the foundation to the ends. Randomly stitch 6-mm Czech beads here and there to create interest and visually tie together the entire strip of beading. Tie off the threads on the back and clip.

▶ Embellish

1 Thread a needle with 18 inches (45.7 cm) of thread. Weave through the donut bezel and exit a cylinder bead in the second or third row from the top of the bezel. Pick up a 6-mm sequin, a 3-mm sequin, and a 15° bead. Skip over the 15° and pass back through the sequins and into the next cylinder bead in the row (figure 2). Repeat this around the entire bezel.

2 Use stop stitch to add a 6-mm sequin, a 3-mm sequin, and a 15° to the tops of the buttons (figure 3).

3 Stitch nail heads to the four corners of the donut, just inside the Czech beads.

▶ Finish

1 When you've completed the beadwork, carefully cut the foundation as close to the beadwork as you can without cutting the threads. Use a dowel or toothpick to roll a thin, even layer of white glue onto the back side of the beaded piece, staying away from the edges of the beadwork and leaving ⅛ inch (3 mm) so that later your needle and thread will glide easily through both layers in the final steps. Place the glue-covered face of the beadwork down against the suede. Allow the glue to dry and then carefully cut the excess suede away flush against the beadwork.

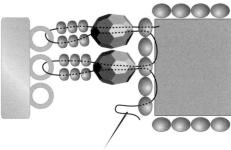

figure 4

2 Stitch a single-bead edging with 11°s the entire way around the cuff. Weave through the beadwork, tie off simple knots, and clip close.

3 If the foundation is too light and shows through the center donut hole, use a black permanent marker to color it.

▶ Clasp

With a doubled thread, pass through an edge bead on either end of the cuff. Pick up one 4-mm Czech bead, three 15°s, one of the loops on the clasp, and three 15°s. Pass back through the Czech bead and into the edge bead you began with. Weave through to the center edge bead and repeat the previous steps, then weave through to the edge bead on the other far side (figure 4) and repeat the previous steps again.

In the manner just described, attach the other half of the clasp to the opposite end of the cuff.

Sherry Serafini
Nicole, 1998
15.2 x 12.7 cm

Seed beads, pearls, crystals,
various embellishment beads;
embroidered, netting stitch

PHOTO BY LARRY SANDERS

Sherry Serafini
Untitled Cuffs, 2008
Approximately 5.1 x 15.2 cm each
Assorted beads; embroidered

PHOTO BY LARRY SANDERS

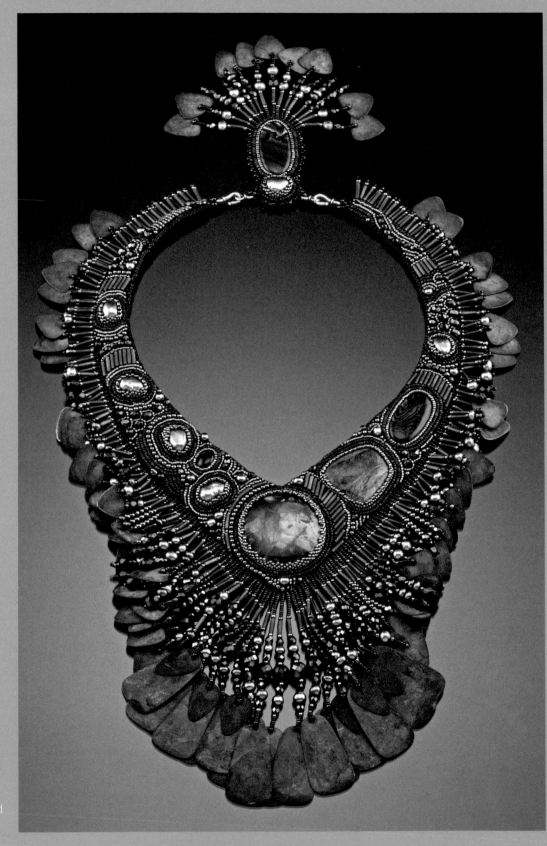

60

Sherry Serafini
Seasons of Wither, 2003
30.5 x 15.2 cm
Assorted beads; embroidered

PHOTO BY LARRY SANDERS

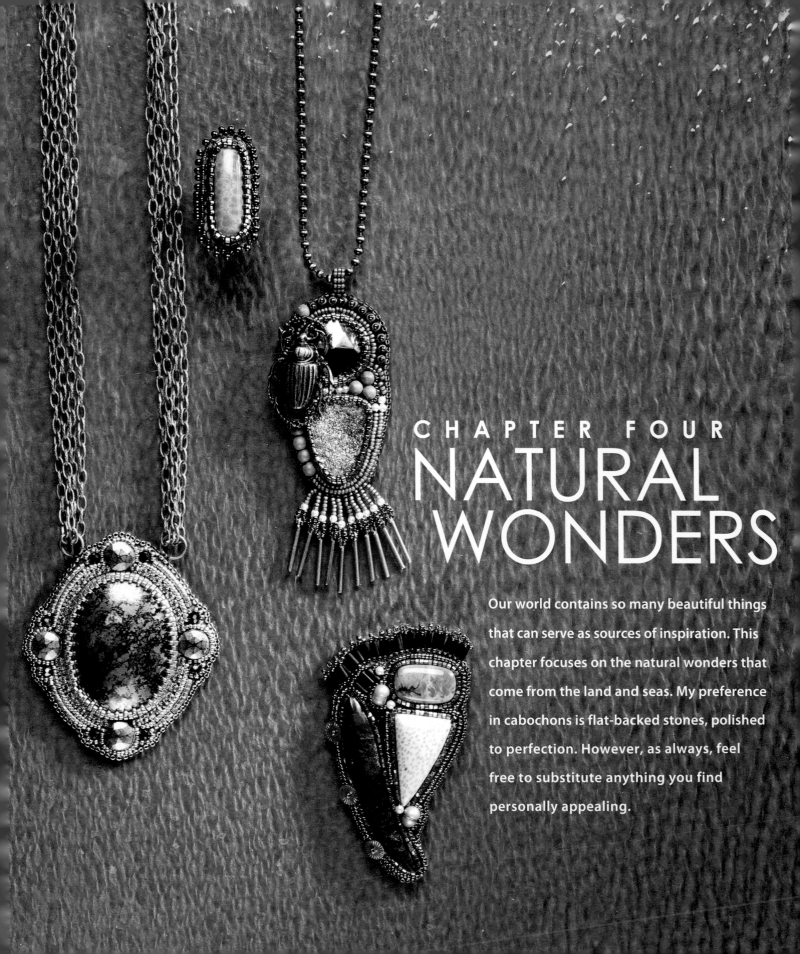

CHAPTER FOUR
NATURAL WONDERS

Our world contains so many beautiful things that can serve as sources of inspiration. This chapter focuses on the natural wonders that come from the land and seas. My preference in cabochons is flat-backed stones, polished to perfection. However, as always, feel free to substitute anything you find personally appealing.

GIVE ME A RING

Rings give you an easy way to flash your embroidered cabochons. A long, thin cabochon is stunning. You can try different shapes as long as they fit comfortably on top of the chosen base. I've kept this ring simple, but you could add crystals to the bezel as well.

▶ Bezel the Cabochon

1 Use industrial-strength adhesive to glue the cabochon to the center of the foundation and allow it to dry.

2 Thread a needle with 1 yd (94.1 cm) of thread and tie a simple knot. Backstitch an even number of cylinder beads around the cabochon. From the back-stitched row, peyote stitch a few rows with the same cylinder beads to form a bezel around the cabochon. When the bezel begins to flare, stitch a final row with 15°s to close the top.

3 Weave through the beadwork, tie off several knots, and clip the thread close. Carefully cut the excess foundation flush against the beadwork. Glue suede to the back of the beadwork with white glue and allow it to dry. Carefully cut the suede flush to the beadwork.

▶ Embellish

1 Thread your needle with 16 inches (40.6 cm) of thread and tie a simple knot. Bury the knot between the beads and the foundation and exit at the edge of the beadwork.

2 Stitch a picot edging using 15°s and 2-mm rounds or 11° seed beads. Stitch all around your beadwork and connect the last bead to the first bead. Weave through the beadwork, tie off several knots, and clip the thread close.

▶ Finish

Put a dab of industrial-strength glue on the pad of the metal ring and let it set up for a few seconds. You'll need enough glue to hold the cabochon in place, but not so much that it seeps out around the beadwork. Push the beadwork onto the pad and allow the glue to dry.

SUPPLIES

Basic Supplies (page 13)

Focal bead:

Coral-colored rectangular cabochon, 7 x 28 mm or similar

Size 11° metallic gold/purple iris cylinder beads, < 1 g

Size 15° metallic gold seed beads, < 1 g

30–40 gunmetal size 11° seed beads or 2-mm round beads

Beading foundation, 2 x 3 inches (5.1 x 7.6 cm)

Suede, 2 x 3 inches (5.1 x 7.6 cm)

1 gold metal adjustable ring with a pad at least 10 mm in diameter

64

Sherry Serafini
Cave Dweller, 2009
33 x 15.2 x 2.5 cm

Crystals, seed beads, drops;
embroidered, embellished

PHOTO BY LARRY SANDERS

FREEFORM BEETLE NECKLACE

Here I've added a metal beetle to create a three-dimensional effect—the beetle seems to be crawling up and over my pendant. Adding dimension to your beadwork with a surprise element such as this one can enhance your design. The cutouts in the beetle allow the beadwork to peek through, adding to the depth.

SUPPLIES

Basic Supplies (page 13)

Focal beads:

> 1 green/gold druzy cabochon,
> 24 mm long*
>
> 1 dark blue/green round crystal
> cabochon, 16–18 mm
>
> 1 brass beetle stamping, 20 x 30 mm

**Size 11° metallic green/gold iris
cylinder beads, 3 g**

Size 15° seed beads:

> Color A, metallic copper, 1 g
> Color B, matte green/purple iris, 1 g

9–11 dusty purple round beads, 4 mm

20–30 white faux round pearls, 2 mm

Size 8° matte burgundy seed beads

10 brass drops, 15 mm long

**Antiqued aluminum ball chain
with closure, 1 yard (94.1 cm)
or desired length**

**Beading foundation, 3 x 5 inches
(76. x 12.7 cm)**

Suede, 3 x 5 inches (76. x 12.7 cm)

*** It should have a tapered shape 18
mm wide at the broadest point, nar-
rowing to 6 mm at the opposite end.**

▶ Bezel the Cabochons

1 Place the druzy and faceted cabochons on a sheet of paper, leaving enough space between them for bezels and at least one row of embroidery. Leaving enough space around the cabochons for several rows of embroidery, sketch a design that you like. Use the fold-in-half method for a symmetrical design, or go with an asymmetrical design. Cut out the design and trace it onto the beading foundation.

2 Glue the druzy and the crystal to the beading foundation with industrial-strength glue according to their placement on the pattern. Allow the glue to dry.

3 Backstitch an even number of cylinder beads around the druzy. From the back-stitched row, work peyote stitch up the sides of the druzy to create a tight bezel. Stitch a final row with 15° A beads to close up the bezel.

4 Repeat step 3 around the crystal.

▶ Embroider

1 Bead embroider around and between the cabochons with 15° Bs, rounds, and pearls. Create texture with stop stitches of size-8° and -15° As. Periodically put the beetle stamping on top of the piece to get a feel for where it should eventually be attached. Embroider 1½ inches (3.8 cm) or so until the pendant is wide enough to accommodate the beetle.

2 When the embroidery is complete, lay the stamping on the designated area and whipstitch around the open areas (the legs are a good place for stitches). If your stamping is large, you may want to use a little industrial-strength glue to tack it down before stitching.

▶ Finish

1 Carefully cut the foundation flush to the beadwork. Glue a piece of suede to the back of the beadwork with white glue.

2 Stitch a single-bead edging with 15° Bs, working carefully around the stamping if it protrudes from the beadwork.

3 Locate the top center 3 edge beads. Create a 3-bead ladder-stitch bail large enough to accommodate the chain.

▶ Fringe

Using the double-needle method, pass thread through the 2 beads on either side of the lower center of the pendant. String five 15° Bs, 1 pearl, four 15° As, 1 drop, and four 15° As. Pass back through the pearl, the 15° Bs, and the edge bead you originally exited.

Repeat until you have the desired amount of fringe—10 fringes are shown here.

Sherry Serafini

Rusted, 2008

61 x 17.8 cm

Seed beads, cabochons by Gary Wilson, metal focal bead by Mary Hettmansperger,
crystals, buttons; embroidered, netting stitch

PHOTO BY LARRY SANDERS

TRIPLE PLAY BROOCH

By doing bead embroidery in just the right colors, these three wildly different cabochons look like they were made for each other. For this heart-stopping creation, each cabochon is first surrounded by a bezel, then embroidery and fringe pull it all together.

69

▶ Design and Embroider

1 Place the focal beads on a sheet of paper in an arrangement you like. To keep the spacing between them able to accommodate beads, leave a space of two cylinder-bead widths between them. I measure this by placing the beads on a needle and holding them between the cabochons. Trace around the stones and then trace a design around those lines. Cut out your pattern.

2 Trace the pattern onto the beading foundation. Using industrial-strength adhesive, glue the cabochons to the foundation according to their placement on the pattern.

Tip: Don't cut the foundation yet. Leave room for your design to "grow."

3 Backstitch with cylinder beads around the cabochons.

continued on next page

SUPPLIES

Basic Supplies (page 13)

Focal beads:

    1 pod-shaped amethyst colored cabochon, 2 x ³⁄₈ inches (5.5 x 1 cm)

    1 triangular spotted goldenrod cabochon, ⁵⁄₈ x 1 inch (16 x 25 mm)

    1 rectangular orange cabochon, ³⁄₈ x ¾ inch (3 x 1.9 cm)

Size 11° metallic gold/purple iris cylinder beads, 1–3 g

Size 15° seed beads:
    Color A, matte black, < 1 g
    Color B, metallic gold, 1–3 g

2 round gold-tone freshwater pearls, 4 mm

3 pink faux pearls, 2 mm

3- or 5-mm matte black bugle beads, 1 g

3 metallic sequins, 6 mm

Beading foundation, 3 x 3 inches (7.6 x 7.6 cm)

1 bar pin back, 1½ inches (3.8 cm) long

Suede, 3 x 3 inches (7.6 x 7.6 cm)

4 Randomly stitch the pearls, some bugles, and some 15°A beads in the spaces between the cabochons. Stitch as many or as few as you like.

5 Stitch around the entire design with 15° Bs.

6 Using stop stitch on top of the beadwork, randomly stitch the sequins where they visually please you.

▶ Finish

1 Carefully cut the foundation flush to the beadwork. Glue the pin back to the beadwork with industrial-strength adhesive.

2 With pointy scissors, cut two small slits in the suede to accommodate the pin back and glue the suede to the back of the beadwork with white glue.

3 Stitch a single-bead edging with 15° Bs all the way around your beadwork. If your thread is too short, weave through the beadwork, tie off simple knots, and begin a new thread. If your thread is long enough, weave to the top of the piece to begin the fringes.

4 Create simple fringe across the top of the brooch with bugle beads and three 15° Bs to make small picots at the top of the bugles. Weave the needle and thread through the beadwork and tie off several knots. Clip close.

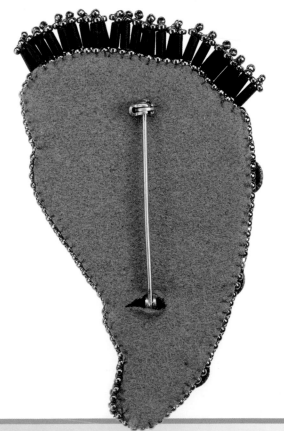

HEAVY-METAL PYRITE PENDANT

Pyrite is a beautiful stone that looks like metal. Paired with silver-toned beads and vintage nail heads and chains, it makes a pendant that's classy, yet has a rock 'n' roll feel. If you prefer a more classic look, use pearls in place of chains.

▶ Bezel around the Cabochon

1 Attach the cabochon to the center of the beading foundation with industrial-strength glue and allow it to dry.

2 Backstitch an even number of cylinder beads around the cabochon. From the backstitched row, work even-count peyote stitch with cylinder beads, creating a bezel. When the bezel begins to flare, stitch a final row with 15°s to close up the top of the bezel.

▶ Embroider around the Bezel

1 Using a ruler, mark the four compass points on your beading foundation around the bezeled stone (figure 1). Backstitch the nail heads at the compass points.

2 Lay the rhinestone chain between the nail heads, scrunching it slightly so the stones are close together but keeping small spaces between the stones for stitching. Cut the length needed.

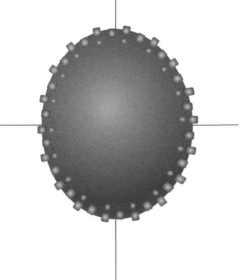

figure 1

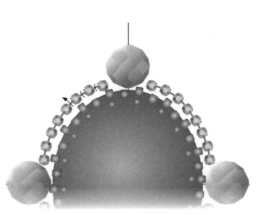

figure 2

3 With a toothpick, spread a smooth layer of industrial-strength adhesive beside the bezel directly on the beading foundation. Lay the chain onto the glue and allow the glue to dry. To ensure that it's securely attached, stitch over the top of the chain between the rhinestones (figure 2). You'll have to force the needle through the adhesive.

4 To tie the entire design together visually, backstitch the 15°s around all of the elements that are in place.

5 Stitch a crystal at the inner corners of each nail head. Stitch a row of 15°s around those.

6 Backstitch with cylinder beads between the crystals to further tie the piece together visually. When you are finished, your work should look like figure 3.

7 Weave the thread to the back of the piece, tie off the threads, and clip the knot.

▶ Finish

1 Carefully cut the foundation so that it's flush with the beadwork.

2 Put the beadwork on the poster board and trace around it. Cut the poster board approximately ⅛ inch (3 mm) smaller than the beadwork. Using white glue, attach the poster board to the back of the beadwork and the suede to the back of the poster board. Allow the glue to dry, and trim the suede flush with the beadwork.

3 Single thread a needle with 18 inches (45.7 cm) of thread and tie a knot. Bury the knot in the beadwork and weave to the edge. Stitch single-bead edging with 15°s the entire way around the beadwork. When your last bead meets your first, attach the 2 together and weave the needle and thread back down through the beadwork, tying off several knots in the beads, and clip the thread close.

▶ Attach the Chains

1 Locate the top-center edge bead of your pendant. Measure over from this point 2 equal distances to find the points to attach the jump rings. Thread 2 needles with 14 inches (35.6 cm) of doubled thread and tie a knot. Bury the knots in the beadwork close to the edge beads you located.

2 Working 1 side at a time, pass the needle through the edge bead and pick up a soldered jump ring. Pass back through the same edge bead and come up through the next edge bead on either side (figure 4). Repeat the thread path for added strength. Weave down through the beadwork and tie off a knot. Clip close. Repeat this step on the other side.

3 Run 2 chains through 1 of the attached jump rings and bring the ends together. Open 1 of the remaining jump rings, slide the 4 chain ends onto the jump ring, and close it up. Repeat on the other side.

4 Attach the clasps to the end jump rings.

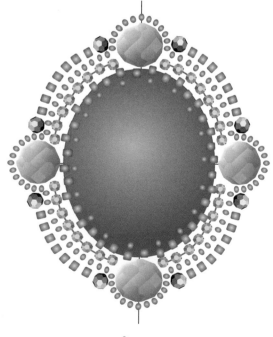

figure 3

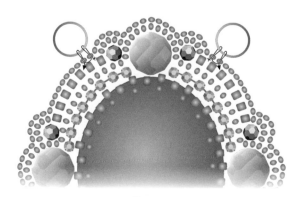

figure 4

FADE
TO GRAY CUFF

The challenge in this elaborate and asymmetrical design lies in choosing which beads to stitch beside each other to allow the monochromatic palette to pop. Refer to chapter 2 for information on color and various finishes.

▶ Design and Embroider

1 Measure out a 1-inch (2.5 cm) lengthwise space on your beading foundation, leaving ¼ inch (6 mm) on both sides. Wrap the foundation around the brass cuff and mark both ends. Do not cut this out because the foundation may shrink a bit when you embroider and you may need a little extra on both ends.

2 Glue the cabochon to the center of the foundation with industrial-strength glue and allow the glue to dry.

continued on next page

continued on next page

SUPPLIES

Basic Supplies (page 13)

Focal bead:
Pear-shaped labradorite cabochon, ¾ inch (1.9 cm) long or less

Size 15° seed beads:
Color A, gunmetal, 3 g
Color B, matte black, 3 g
Color C, opaque gray, 3 g

3-mm metallic blue/purple iris bugle beads, 3 g

5 pink iris flower rondelles, 6 mm

2 jet-black crystal rounds, 6 mm

40–50 silver freshwater pearls, 6 mm

90–100 hematite beads, 3 mm

Size 11° gunmetal seed beads, 2 g

1 brass cuff, 1 inch (2.5 cm) wide

Beading foundation, 1½ x 8 inches (3.8 x 20.3 cm)

Suede, 1½ x 8 inches (3.8 x 20.3 cm)

3 Backstitch with 15° A beads around the cabochon. Try to keep an even number. (You may end up with an odd count, depending on the shape of your stone.) From the backstitched row, work even- or odd-count peyote stitch with 15° As, creating a bezel around the focal bead. At the pointed spot of the cab, you may need to pass through 2 beads in the bezel to close it up tightly (figure 1).

figure 1

4 With the focal bead as your guide, begin bead embroidery around the cabochon, taking care to stay within the marked lines. If it helps you with design, draw lines with a permanent marker indicating where you'd like the beads to go. Use any or all of the remaining embellishment beads, reserving the 11's for finishing. Work out from the focal point, approaching the ends of the cuff last. Let some of the beads go on road trips (page 26). Stitch bugle beads on one side and a row of hematite beads on the other side. Use the stop stitch technique with some of the hematite beads. Try to balance the shades of gray as well as the matte and shiny finishes. Check your progress periodically by wrapping the beadwork around the form. Keep the ends of the cuff simple—this part of the cuff will

be under your wrist, and embellishment beads that are too bulky will be uncomfortable to wear.

▶ **Finish**

1 After the cuff has been beaded to your satisfaction, check that all of your stitches are secure and that you have enough embroidery to reach the ends.

2 Carefully cut the foundation flush with the beadwork.

3 Attach the suede to the backside of the brass cuff with white glue, keeping the glue away from the edges, and allow it to dry. Trim the suede to approximately ¹⁄₁₆ inch (1.6 mm) from the edge all the way around.

4 Attach the beadwork to the top of the brass cuff with white glue, keeping the glue away from the edges to allow for stitching later.

5 Single thread a needle with 24 inches (61 cm) of thread and tie a knot. Weave through the beadwork to bury the knot and exit at the edge. Stitch single-bead edging with 11's all the way around the cuff. When your last bead meets your first, attach the 2 together and weave the needle and thread back down through the beadwork, tying off several knots in the beads, and clip the thread close.

ROCK STAR CUFF

In this cool design, instead of one focal point, you'll work with many, embellishing with embroidery after capturing each cabochon in a bezel. Let your imagination go wild, and use any color or shape—square, oval, or round—that appeals to you. You can also make this cuff narrower by creating only the middle section.

SUPPLIES

Basics Supplies (page 13)

Focal bead:
> Odd- or pear-shaped labradorite cabochon, no wider than ¾ inch (1.9 cm)

6–8 dark mossy green oval cabochons, 13 x 10 mm

16–20 gold-tone square cabochons, ½ inch (13 mm)

Size 11° cylinder beads:
> Color A, black, 5 g
> Color B, gold metallic iris, 8 g

Size 15° gold metallic seed beads, 10 g

140–160 seed and freshwater pearls, 3–4 mm

20–30 vintage sew-on rhinestones, crystals, and nail heads

14 dark gray/black crystal rounds, 2 mm

Size 11° gold metallic seed beads, 5 g

Beading foundation, 3½ x 8 inches (8.9 x 20.3 cm)

2 hook-and-eye sets

Suede, 3½ x 8 inches (8.9 x 20.3 cm)

77

figure 1

▶ Measure and Design

1 Refer to figure 1 as you do steps 1 and 2. The width of the cuff will be determined by the sizes of the cabochons. Begin by drawing a line horizontally and one vertically through the center of the beading foundation. Place your focal bead at the intersection, and then put the oval cabochons across the longer line, leaving a ⅛-inch (3 mm) space between them and on both sides of the focal bead. Draw around them so you know where they'll be glued.

2 Place a row of square cabochons on both sides of the center row, leaving a ⅛-inch (3 mm) space between them and the center cabochons and between each other, and trace them onto the foundation. Remove the cabochons from the beading foundation and measure an extra ⅛ inch (3 mm) from the outer cabochons, then draw lines indicating the long edges of the cuff.

3 To determine the length, wrap the piece of beading foundation around your wrist and make marks where one end meets the other. Subtract ¼ inch (6 mm) for the hook-and-eye closures, and draw lines perpendicular to the edges drawn in the previous step, to indicate the cuff ends. Glue all the cabochons into place with industrial-strength adhesive and allow the glue to dry.

▶ Embroider

1 Thread a needle with 1 yard (91.4 cm) of thread and tie a knot. Start at one end of the cuff with A cylinder beads and backstitch, one cabochon at a time, attaching an even number of beads around all the cabochons in the middle row.

2 Work 2 rounds of peyote stitch with the same cylinder beads off the back-stitched rounds, to form bezels around the cabochons. When the bezel starts to flare out, stitch a final row with 15°s to close up around the cabochon. Repeat for every cabochon.

3 Repeat steps 1 and 2 with the square cabochons, using B cylinder beads and the same 15°s.

4 When all the cabochons are completely bezeled, randomly backstitch embellishments of pearls and vintage beads in the spaces between the cabochons.

5 Backstitch one 2-mm crystal in each space between the square cabochons along the outer edges.

► Finish

1 Carefully cut the foundation flush against the beadwork.

2 Stitch the hook and eye closures to the underside of the beadwork at the ends, making sure they aligned on each side.

3 Attach the suede to the back of the beadwork with white glue. Once the glue is dry, trim the suede flush to the foundation.

4 Stitch single-bead edging with 11°s all the way around the cuff. When the first edge bead meets the last, weave the needle and thread through the beadwork, tie off several small knots, and clip close.

Sherry Serafini
Crystal Eyes, 2007
22.9 x 15.2 cm
Assorted beads; embroidered
PHOTO BY LARRY SANDERS

ARIZONA SUNSET EARRINGS

Beautiful Southwestern skies are the inspiration for the intoxicating hues used in these earrings. The colorful cabochons and drops combine with a simple palette of seed beads to make a bold statement.

Make 2

▶ Design and Embroider

1 Draw horizontal and vertical lines through the center of the foundation to serve as guidelines. Place the focal beads on the foundation and play with the arrangement, allowing room for 2 rows of 15°s between the top nail head and the center cabochon, and 1 row of pearls and 2 rows of 15°s between the center and bottom cabochons. I like to string the beads that will go between the cabochons on a needle and put them temporarily between the cabochons to make sure they'll fit. Trace around the 3 focal beads then glue them to the foundation with industrial-strength adhesive.

2 Backstitch a row of 15°s around all of the cabochons.

3 At the corners of the top square and the middle cabochon, backstitch a 4-mm crystal sequin, then backstitch with 15°s around the crystals to tie the unit together (figure 1).

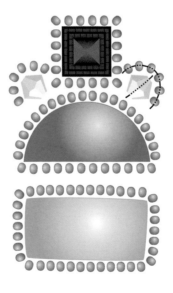

figure 1

continued on next page

SUPPLIES

Basic Supplies (page 13)

Focal beads:

    2 coral half-moon cabochons, 10 x 20 mm

    2 spotted goldenrod rectangular cabochons, 10 x 20 mm

2 square brass nail heads with prongs cut off, 8 mm

Size 15° bronze seed beads, 3 g

62–80 pale green AB crystal bicones, 4 mm

14 copper pearls, 3 mm

6 copper crystal sequins, 4 mm

Size 11° black cylinder beads, 3 g

4 size 11° bronze seed beads

40–60 copper crystal sequins, 2 mm

2-mm crystal bicones:

    Color A, topaz, 64–80
    Color B, mocha, 30–42
    Color C, pale green AB, 16–24

22–34 turquoise, bronze, and brass metal drops, 10–30 mm

2 turquoise stone drops, 20 mm

2 pieces of beading foundation, each 3 x 2 inches (7.6 x 5.1 cm)

2 fishhook ear wires

2 pieces of suede, each 3 x 2 inches (7.6 x 5.1 cm)

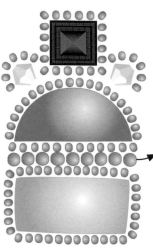

figure 2

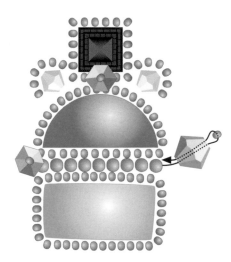

figure 3

4 Backstitch a row of pearls between the middle and bottom cabochon (figure 2).

   5 Do a stop stitch with the sequins and 15°s at the ends of these rows and between the center of the nail head and the middle cabochon (figure 3).

6 Tie off your thread on the back with simple knots. Carefully cut the excess foundation flush against the beadwork and attach the suede to the back with white glue. After the glue is dry, cut the excess suede flush against the beadwork.

7 Thread a needle with 18 inches (45.7 cm) of thread. Begin at the top, where the ear wire will be attached, and stitch a single-bead edging with cylinder beads.

► **Attach the Ear Wire**

1 Refer to figure 4 as you work steps 1, 2, and the first half of 3. Locate the top 3 center edge beads and pass the needle through 1 of the beads on either side of the center. Pick up 2 cylinder beads, one 11° seed bead, the ear wire, one 11° seed bead, and 2 more cylinders. Pass the needle down through the cylinder bead on the opposite side of the center bead.

2 Pass the needle up through the cylinder bead beside the one just exited. Pick up 3 cylinders. Pass through the 11°, the ear wire and the 11°. Pick up 3 more cylinders and pass down through the cylinder in the edge row beside the one you began with.

3 Weave back through all of the beads added in step 2 again, for strength. Weave through the beading foundation or under the beads and exit the center bead. Pick up a 4-mm crystal and pass through the loop of the ear finding, back down through the crystal and the center edge bead. Repeat the thread path, for strength. Pass the needle and thread through the beadwork, tie off several small knots, and clip close.

► Fringe

1 Using the double-needle method, add fringe by following the chart (figure 5). Depending on the size of your cabochons and the number of edge beads you've attached, of course, you'll need either more or less fringe than appears on the earrings shown, so use my pattern just as a guide.

2 At the last edge bead in the row, use one of the working threads to make a strand of fringe that will run across the top of the existing fringe. Pick up the desired amount of beads or follow the chart and pass the needle and thread up through the edge bead on the other side of the fringe (figure 6). With the other needle, pass back through the strand from the opposite side. Weave through all the fringe again for strength.

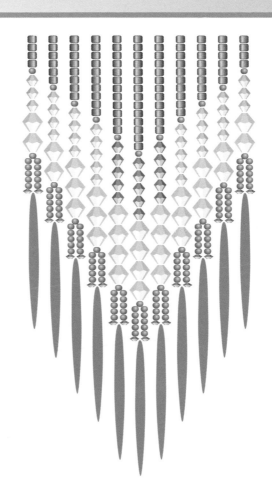

figure 5

figure 4

figure 6

CLASSIC COLLAR

Pull out all the stops with this intricately embroidered collar. Use backstitch, scalloping, cross hatch, stop stitch, and single-bead edging to complement the focal cabochon. Drop beads create deep texture, and the simple fringe makes this collar a classic.

▶ Pattern

1 Draw a circular shape on a piece of paper to accommodate your neck size (page 24). Place your focal bead down in the center and trace around it, then determine the width of the necklace by allowing for a row of 15°s and a row of 11°s around it. Play with the shape of the necklace, tapering to ⅜ inch (1 cm) at the ends. Fold the paper in half and cut the pattern out. Or you can use the template provided on page 86.

2 Trace the pattern onto the foundation, then glue the cabochon onto the foundation with industrial-strength adhesive and allow it to dry.

▶ Set the Cabochon

Backstitch around the cabochon with an even number of 15° A beads. Using 15° As, peyote stitch off the backstitched row up the side of the cabochon, to create a bezel.

continued on next page

Basic Supplies (page 13)

Focal bead:
Cream oval cabochon,
30 x 22 mm or smaller

Size 15° seed beads:
  Color A, bronze, 10 g
  Color B, metallic
    purple/gold iris, 10 g
  Color C, pale green, 10 g

Size 11° seed beads:
  Color A, bronze, 2 g
  Color D, matte
    purple/gold iris, 10 g

17–21 dusty lavender drop beads, 4 mm

3-mm color D bugle beads, matte purple/gold iris, 5 g

4-mm round beads:
  50 color C, pale green
  16–20 color E,
    dark metallic purple

Size 8° color D seed beads, matte purple/gold iris, 3 g

14–18 bronze pearls, 6 mm

13 color B bugle beads, metallic purple/gold iris, 30 mm

15 color B Czech beads, metallic purple/gold iris, 6 mm

1 smoky fancy round glass bead, 14 mm

Beading foundation 8½ x 11 inches (21.6 x 27.9 cm)

Suede 8½ x 11 inches (21.6 x 27.9 cm)

1 gold toggle clasp

85

▶ Embroider

Let the fun begin! Start embroidering out from the cabochon. You can draw a design or just let the beads tell you where to go as you stitch. Take the beads on little road trips (page 26) across the design—this is what keeps it cohesive and well balanced. Play with all of the basic stitches, including stop stitch, and scallop stitch. Backstitch the drop beads in groups of 3 or more, and stitch curved rows with bugle beads. Accent the shapes with seed beads. When you get to the narrow ends of the collar, stitch simple designs with seed bead crosshatch stitching and perhaps 1 or 2 of the 4-mm round beads as accents.

▶ Finish

1 When you've completely beaded your collar to your satisfaction, carefully cut the excess beading foundation flush against the beadwork. Glue the suede onto the back beadwork with white glue and allow it to dry. Carefully cut the excess suede flush to the beading foundation.

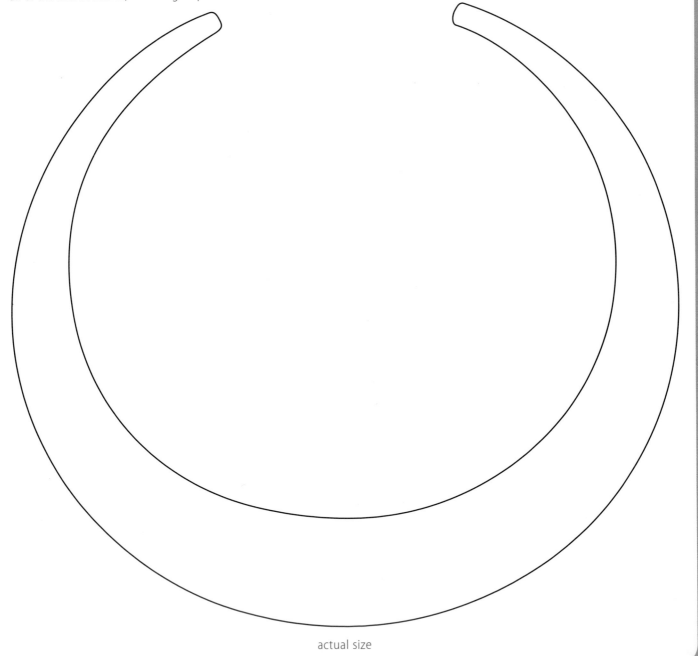

actual size

figure 1

2 Stitch a single-bead edging around the entire design with 11°s.

▶ Add the Clasp

Double-thread a needle with 18 inches (45.7 cm) of thread, so you have 9 inches (22.9 cm) on each side, and tie a knot. Weave through the beadwork, hiding the knot, and exit one of the edge beads at the back of the neckpiece, where the clasp will go. String two 11°s, 1 color C 4-mm round bead, 4 to six 11°s, 1 piece of the clasp, and 4 to six 11°s. Pass back through the 4-mm round, pick up two 11°s and go through the edge bead next to the one you originally exited (figure 1). Repeat the thread path at least twice more to ensure a secure clasp. Attach the other half of the clasp to the opposite end in the same way.

▶ Fringe

1 Using the double-needle method, thread 2 needles on a 3-yard (2.7 m)

length of thread. Locate the edge bead at the bottom center of the neckpiece and use it as the starting point. Following my pattern (shown in figure 2), or making up your own, string your first strand of fringe and bring both needles up through the center edge bead. Pass one needle down through the edge bead on the right and the other down through the edge bead on the left. Make 5 to 6 rows of fringe on each side of the center.

2 With the needles exiting downward through the edge beads next to the outer rows of fringe, string the loop that swoops across the front of the fringe. To do so, pick up the beads for the loop (figure 3) with one of the needles and pass up through the edge bead on the opposite side of the fringe. Pass the other needle through the strand from the opposite direction.

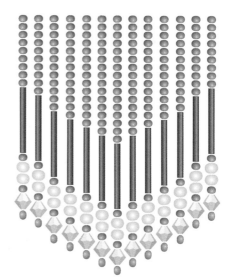

figure 2

figure 3

BLACK WIDOW COLLAR

This collar is a great one for practicing with a monochromatic color scheme and texture. It's created almost entirely with stop stitches. The fun beads include a variety of rounds and vintage nail heads.

▶ The Base

1 Create a pattern by drawing a circular shape on a piece of paper to accommodate your neck size. Place your focal beads down in the center, leaving ¾ inch (1.9 cm) above the top cabochon and ¼ inch (6 mm) between them for a few rows of embroidery. Trace around the beads then play with the shape of the front of the necklace, allowing another ¼ inch (6 mm) around the focal beads for embroidery. Taper the ends to ⅜ inch (1 cm). When you're pleased with the design, fold the paper in half and cut the pattern out. Or you can use the template provided on page 92.

2 Trace the pattern onto the foundation. Glue the cabochons onto the foundation with industrial-strength adhesive and allow it to dry.

3 This next part is a little tricky. Lay the chain along the inner edge of the design and use wire cutters to cut the length needed. Using a toothpick, start at the top right or left of the inner edge and apply a narrow strip of industrial-strength adhesive 1 inch (2.5 cm) long. Lay the first inch (2.5 cm) of the ball chain on the adhesive and allow the adhesive to dry. Continue in 1-inch (2.5 cm) increments until the entire length of chain is glued to the inner edge.

4 Repeat step 3 twice more for 2 more rows of ball chain, allowing the adhesive to dry thoroughly between each ball chain segment.

5 Thread a needle with 1 yard (91.4 cm) of thread and tie a knot at the end. Pass the needle and thread up through the beadwork at one end of the neckpiece, between the chains. Make tiny stitches between the balls of the chains (figure 1).

continued on next page

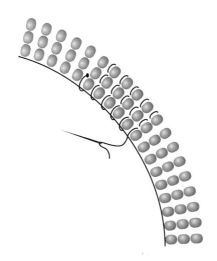

figure 1

SUPPLIES

Basic Supplies (page 13)

Focal beads:
    1 teardrop-shaped ammonite cabochon, 20–32 mm
    1 round black onyx cabochon, 20–24 mm

2-mm gunmetal ball chain, approximately 4 ft (1.2 m)

Size 11° black opaque seed beads, 30 g

Size 15° seed beads:
    Color A matte black, 10 g
    Color B gunmetal, 10 g
    Color C dark brown iris, 10 g

2 gross of hematite round beads, 2 mm (reserve 88 for fringe)

25–30 black round crystals, 6 mm

2 gross of dark smoky round crystals, 4 mm (reserve 88 for fringe)

2 gross of black AB bicone crystals, 3 mm (reserve 88 for fringe)

Fun beads: 4-mm rounds, 4-mm nail heads, etc.

Bugle beads, 16 mm:
    8 matte black twisted
    18 gunmetal

Beading foundation, 8½ x 11 inches (21.6 x 27.9 cm)

Wire cutters

Suede, 8½ x 11 inches (21.6 x 27.9 cm)

1 silver triple-loop clasp with or without extension chain

89

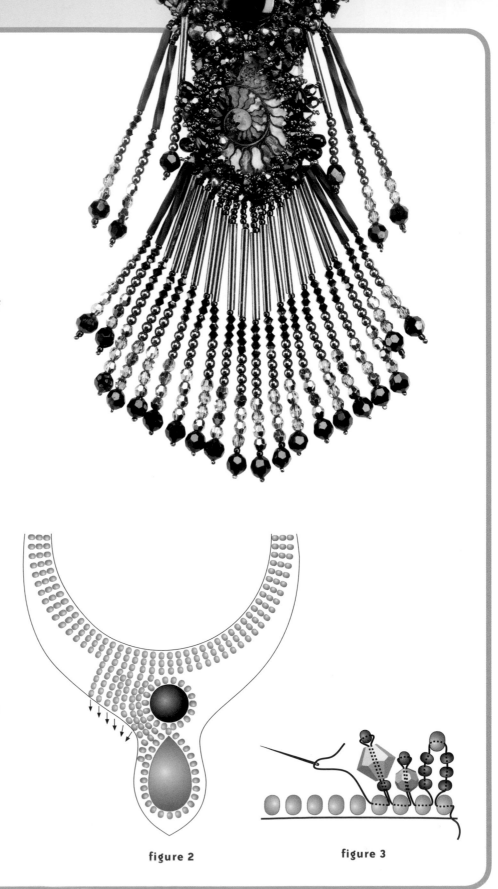

6 Backstitch with 11°s over the entire foundation, first backstitching around the cabochons and then forming vertical rows where the sections meet (figure 2). This embroidery will all be covered with more embellishment so it doesn't have to be a work of art. It serves to keep the piece flexible.

▶ Embroider

1 The rest of the design is done in stop stitches. Randomly choose rounds, crystals, and fun beads and create stop stitches with 15°s. Stitch random loops of 15°s across the entire design (figure 3).

2 Backstitch nail heads at evenly spaced increments on top of the ball chain, between the 2 longer rows.

▶ Finish

1 After you've completely beaded the collar to your satisfaction, carefully cut the excess beading foundation flush with the beadwork. Attach the beadwork to the piece of suede with white glue and allow it to dry. Carefully cut the excess suede flush with the beading foundation.

2 Using 11°s, stitch a single-bead edging around the entire design.

▶ Add the Clasp

Double thread a needle with 18 inches (45.7 cm) of thread so you have 9 inches (22.9 cm) on each side, and tie a knot. Weave through the beadwork, hiding the knot, and exit one of the edge beads at the back of the neckpiece where the clasp will go. String four 11°s, 1 of the rings of the clasp, and four 11°s. Pass back through the edge bead you originally exited. Weave

figure 2

figure 3

through the beadwork to exit the edge bead that accommodates the next loop on the clasp and attach it the same way. Repeat this process with the third loop. Repeat the thread path at least twice more to ensure a secure attachment. Attach the other half of the clasp to the opposite end in the same way.

▶ Fringe

1 Using the double-needle method, thread 2 needles on a 3-yard (2.7 m) length of thread. Locate the 2 edge beads at the bottom center of the neckpiece. Choose the one to the right or the left to begin the fringe. **Note:** If you don't have 2 centered edge beads, simply work with the one you have and adjust the fringe to accommodate.

2 Following my pattern (figure 4) or making up your own, string your first strand of fringe and bring both needles up through the edge bead. Pass 1 needle down through the edge bead on the right and the other down through the edge bead on the left. Continue your fringe as desired.

3 Weave through all the fringe again, for added strength.

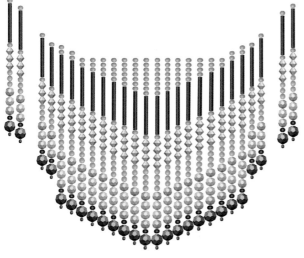

figure 4

Sherry Serafini
Mantis, 2006
30.5 x 16.5 cm
Assorted beads; embroidered
PHOTO BY LARRY SANDERS

actual size

CHAPTER FIVE
GOTTA HAVE BLING!

Sparkle and bling—who doesn't love it? This chapter is all about the flash of crystals. Small or large, round or bicone, these little gems catch and reflect light like nothing else. Wear them and light up any room.

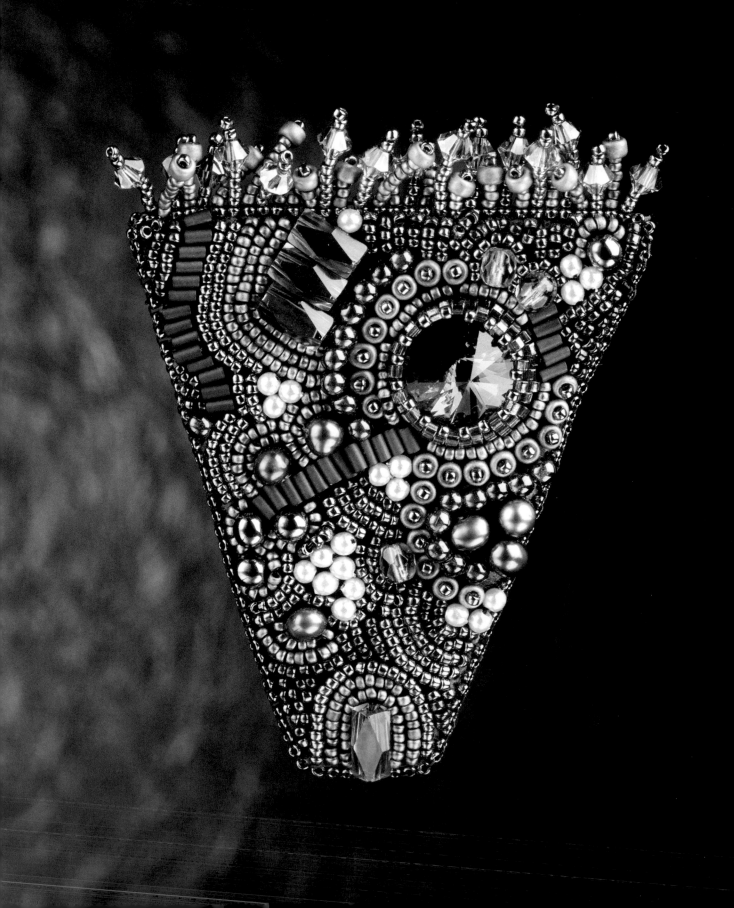

RIVOLI BROOCH

This wonderful project makes the most of beads left over from other projects. Choose a focal rivoli, and then select a variety of shapes and sizes to coordinate with it. Follow your heart, and the bead paths and clusters that please you.

▶ Design and Set Rivoli

1 Cut the brooch pattern from a sheet of paper using the top template on page 96, or create your own design. Cut a circle for the rivoli's position using the small round template on page 96.

2 Trace your pattern onto the beading foundation. Determine where you'd like to place your rivoli and trace the circle pattern there. Cut the circle out on the line, not outside it, or the rivoli could fall through the hole. Apply industrial-strength adhesive to the edges of the rivoli and position it in the cutout, cleaning up any glue that seeps out around the edges. While the glue dries, balance the foundation with the rivoli on top of something, such as a small drinking glass, to keep the rivoli straight.

3 Single thread your needle with approximately 1 yd (91.4 cm) of thread and tie a knot. Backstitch an even number of cylinder beads around the rivoli. From the backstitched row, work 1 row of peyote stitch with the cylinder beads to form a bezel. Work a final row with 15° A beads to close up around the rivoli and hold it in place.

▶ Embroider

Begin bead embroidery with the remaining beads, reserving fourteen 8°s, the crystal bicones, and some 15° As and Cs for fringe. Create beaded paths throughout the design. Stop stitch 8°s with 15° Cs. You have the option of drawing your designs or letting the beads guide you as you stitch.

continued on next page

SUPPLIES

Basic Supplies (page 13)

Focal bead:
    1 amber crystal rivoli, 14 mm

Size 11° metallic gold cylinder beads, 1 g

Size 8° matte green/gold seed beads, 1 g

16–20 dusty pink bicone crystals, 4 mm

Size 15° seed beads:
    Color A metallic gold, 5 g
    Color B metallic purple/blue iris, 5 g
    Color C matte green/gold, 5 g

2–3-mm matte dark bronze bugle beads, 1 g

Fun beads:
    Pink round pearls, 2mm
    Purple round beads, 3 mm
    Gold-lined green round crystals, 4 mm
    Gold and copper round beads, 4–5 mm
    Clear AB polygon crystals, 8 mm

Beading foundation, 4 x 4 inches (10 x 10 cm)

Poster board, 4 x 4 inches (10 x 10 cm)

1 pin back, 1½ inches (3.8 cm)

Suede, 4 x 4 inches (10 x 10 cm)

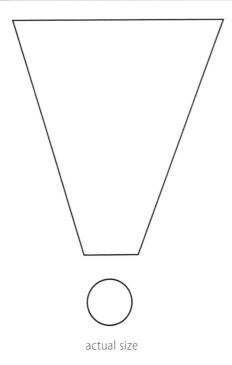

actual size

▶ Finish

1 When your brooch is beaded to your satisfaction, tie off knots on the back and clip the threads. Cut the excess beading foundation flush against the beadwork.

2 Trace the brooch pattern onto the poster board and cut it slightly smaller than the beadwork. Attach this to the back of the beadwork with white glue.

3 Attach the pin back to the poster board with industrial strength-glue and allow it to dry. Cut slits in the suede to accommodate the ends of the pin back. Fit the suede over the open finding and glue it to the poster board with white glue. Trim the suede flush with the beadwork.

4 Single thread your needle with 1 yard (91.4 cm) of thread and tie a knot. Begin at the top of the brooch, where fringe will be added, and connect the pieces together by working a single-bead edging with 15°s all the way around the brooch.

▶ Fringe

Create short, random fringe using the bicone crystals, 15°s, and 8°s. Weave the needle through the beadwork, tie off several knots, and clip close.

Sherry Serafini
Serenity, 2007
30.5 x 19 cm
Assorted beads; embroidered
PHOTO BY LARRY SANDERS

SUPPLIES

Basic Supplies (page 13)

Focal bead:
   Pale blue round flat-back
   crystal cabochon,
   12–16 mm

Size 11° metallic pink cylinder
beads, 2 g

Size 15° silver seed beads, 2 g

2 pink AB chatons with metal
settings, 8–10 mm

17–19 white round faux pearls,
2 mm

Beading foundation,
2 x 3 inches (5.1 x 7.6 cm)

Suede, 2 x 3 inches
(5.1 x 7.6 cm)

1 adjustable ring with a pad
at least 10 mm in diameter

BLING RING

**Rings are fun! I call these instant gratification gems. Pick a flat-back crystal
in your favorite color and generate some exciting adornment for your finger!**

▶ Bezel the Cabochon

1 Attach the large crystal cabochon to
the center of the beading foundation with
industrial-strength glue and allow it to dry.

2 Thread a needle with 1 yard (91.4 cm)
of thread and tie a simple knot. Backstitch an even number of cylinder beads
around the cabochon. From the backstitched row, work several rows of peyote
stitch with the cylinder beads, forming
a bezel around the cabochon. When the
bezel begins to flare out, work a final row
of peyote stitch with 15°s to close up
around the top.

continued on next page

▶ Add Chatons and Embroider

1 Backstitch the chatons flush against both sides of your bezeled cabochon. The settings should have holes on the underside that you can stitch through. If you find that they bobble after they're sewn, simply use a toothpick to add a dab of industrial strength glue to the bottom centers.

2 Backstitch a row of 15°s around the entire piece to tie it together visually. You should have enough thread left over to continue into the embellishment of the bezel.

3 Weave through the second cylinder-bead row of peyote stitch from the top and pick up 1 pearl and one 15°. Skip over the 15° and pass back through the pearl and into the next cylinder bead in the peyote row (figure 1). Continue around the entire bezel in this manner.

4 Weave through the beadwork, tie off several knots on the back of the beading foundation, and clip the thread close.

▶ Finish

1 Carefully cut the excess foundation flush against your beadwork. Attach the

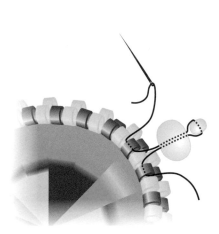

figure 1

Sherry Serafini
Lady Rocks, 2010
16.5 x 10.2 x 2.5 cm
Cabochons, crystals, drops, pearls, plastic; embroidered

suede to the back of the beadwork with white glue and allow it to dry.

2 Rethread your needle with 16 inches (40.6 cm) of thread and tie a simple knot. Bury the knot under the beadwork and exit at the edge of the beadwork. Stitch a single-bead edging with 15°s all the way around your beadwork, connecting your last bead to your first. Weave through the beadwork, tie off several knots between the beads, and clip the thread close.

3 Put a dab of industrial-strength glue on the pad of the metal ring—enough glue to hold the cabochon in place, but not so much that it seeps out around the beadwork—and let it set up for a few seconds. Push the beadwork onto the pad and allow it to dry.

Sherry Serafini
Under the Boardwalk, 2008
35.6 x 12.7 x 0.6 cm
Cabochons, seed beads, pearls, shells, wooden discs; embroidered
PHOTO BY LARRY SANDERS

FAN-SHAPED RIVOLI EARRINGS

A Japanese fan, gifted to me by a wonderful friend from Japan, provided the inspiration for these elegant earrings. Make several pairs and present them to your terrific friends, wherever they may be!

Make 2

▶ Design and Embroider

1 Using either my template (below) or creating your own design, draw your pattern on a piece of paper and cut it out.

actual size

2 Trace the pattern onto both pieces of beading foundation. Cut the center circle out on the line, not outside it, because otherwise the rivoli might fall through the hole. Do not cut out the earring shapes because your beads could be slightly bigger than my pattern and you may need to accommodate the difference. Or you may feel creative and want to add more beads to the earrings!

continued on next page

SUPPLIES

Basic Supplies (page 13)

Focal beads:
    2 rose AB crystal
    rivolis, 14 mm

Size 11° metallic gold cylinder beads, 1 g

Size 15° metallic gold seed beads, 3 g

24–26 white faux pearls, 3 mm

28–30 lavender round beads, 4 mm

2 topaz crystal drops, 7 x 15 mm (shown here) or 5 x 7 mm

2 pieces of beading foundation, each 3 x 3 inches (7.6 x 7.6 cm)

2 pieces of suede, each 3 x 3 inches (7.6 x 7.6 cm)

2 French ear wires

Flat nose pliers

101

Apply industrial-strength adhesive to the edges of the rivoli and position it in the cutout, cleaning up any glue that seeps out around the edges. While the glue dries, balance the foundation with the rivoli on top of something, such as a small drinking glass, to keep the rivoli straight.

3 Single thread a needle with 1 yard (91.4 cm) of thread and tie a knot. Backstitch an even number of cylinder beads around the rivoli. From the backstitched row, work 1 row of peyote stitch with cylinder beads. Peyote stitch a final row with 15°s to close up around the rivoli and hold it in place.

4 Backstitch 3-mm pearls around the lower half of the bezeled rivoli, then backstitch 4-mm beads around the pearls.

▶ Finish

1 Tie off the knots on the back and clip the threads. Cut the excess beading foundation flush with the beadwork.

2 Using flat nose pliers, bend the loop of the French ear wire so it lies flat against the back of the beadwork. Whip stitch this into place, making sure the top of the ear wire is almost flush with the top of the actual beadwork (figure 1).

3 Glue the suede to the back of the earring with industrial-strength adhesive, covering the wire; using industrial-strength adhesive will keep the wire from moving between the backing and the beadwork and ensure that the earrings always sit properly when worn. Trim the excess suede flush with the beadwork.

4 Single thread your needle with 1 yard (91.4 cm) of thread and tie a knot. Beginning at the bottom center, where the drop will be added later, work a picot edging with 15°s through both layers all the way around the earring. When your last bead meets your first, connect the two. You're in position to create the drop without starting a new thread.

▶ Drop

Pass your needle through the edge bead and through the picot to the right or left of the center picot. Pick up four 15°s, 1 pearl, six 15°s, 1 drop, six 15°s. Pass back through the pearl, pick up four 15°s, and pass through the picot on the opposite side of the center picot and up through an edge bead (figure 2). Repeat the thread path for added strength.

figure 1

figure 2

SUPPLIES

Basic Supplies (page 13)

Focal beads:
  1 purple/red
  crystal triangle, 27 mm

  1 goldenrod round glass
  cabochon, 10 mm

  5 purple glass
  disk-like beads, 6 mm

**Size 11° metallic purple/gold
iris cylinder beads, 5 g**

Size 15° seed beads:
  Color A, metallic gold, 10 g
  Color B, matte
  burgundy, 10 g
  Color C, matte black, 10 g

Fun beads:
  2–3-mm matte blue iris
  bugle beads, 10 g

  34–40 golden
  seed pearls, 4 mm

  12–20 blue AB Czech
  fire-polished beads, 5 mm

  Size 11° metallic
  purple hex beads, 10 g

  6–10 purple/red AB
  crystal sequins, 5 mm

**Size 11° gold metallic
seed beads, 5 g**

**1 gross of matte blue iris
magatama drops, 4 mm**

1 wavy brass bracelet blank

**Suede, 3 x 7 inches
(7.6 x 17.8 cm)**

Beading foundation:
  2 x 2 inches (5.1 x 5.1 cm)
  3 x 7 inches (7.6 x 17.8 cm)

ROCKIN' WAVY CUFF

I had the pleasure of spending Mardi Gras with friends in Louisiana, and this piece reflects the wild colors of that weekend. Working with two separate pieces of beading foundation allows the pointed-back stone to be raised up slightly, providing a cushion.

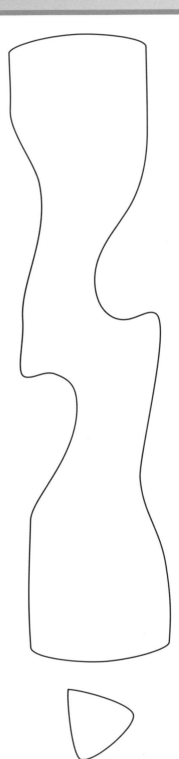

actual size

▶ Prepare Cuff and Patterns

1 Use a dowel to roll a thin layer of white glue on the underside of the brass cuff, the part that will be against your skin. Carefully glue the suede to the cuff, leaving excess suede overlapping the edges. Smooth out any air pockets between the brass and the suede with your fingers. When the glue is dry, carefully cut the suede to approximately 1/16 inch (1.6 mm) all the way around. Set aside.

2 Make a photocopy of the wavy cuff and the triangle templates (top left and bottom left respectively) and cut them out. Trace the cuff pattern onto the larger piece of foundation. Don't cut it out just yet; you'll do that later.

▶ Bezel and Set the Triangle

1 Trace the triangle template onto the smaller piece of beading foundation and cut away the interior shape on the lines, not outside them, because the stone could fall through the hole. Apply industrial-strength adhesive to the edges of the triangle stone and position it in the cutout, cleaning up any glue that seeps out around the edges. While the glue dries, balance the foundation with the stone on top of a drinking glass to keep the stone straight.

2 Backstitch an even number of cylinder beads around the triangle. From the backstitched row, peyote stitch 2 rows of cylinder beads, creating a bezel around the stone. Peyote stitch a final row of 15°s to close up the top of the bezel. ***Note:*** You can stitch another round of 15°s if your beadwork is loose and the beads aren't tight around the triangle.

3 Weave down through the beadwork to the back side of the foundation and tie off several knots. Carefully cut the excess foundation away from your triangle, leaving a 1/16-inch (1.6 mm) edge for stitching.

4 Place the triangle in the desired position on the cuff foundation (figure 1) and trace around it. Draw a small circle—I suggest you trace around a small coin—in the middle of the drawn triangle shape and cut this out.

5 The circle cut in the previous step serves as a place to insert the back point of the triangle stone and creates a cushion for the stone. Attach the bezeled triangle stone to the the newly cut hole with industrial-strength glue, gluing around the hole, not through it. When this has dried, whip stitch the ¹⁄₁₆-inch (1.6 mm) edges of the triangle to the cuff foundation (figure 2).

▶ Embroider

1 Embroider the rest of your cuff with the remaining beads, reserving the 11° seed beads and magatamas for finishing. Glue any smaller focal stones to the foundation with industrial-strength adhesive and bead around them. Use all the stitches discussed in chapter 2 and remember to take your beads on road trips (page 26) throughout the entire design. Make sure you keep your tension even and stay inside the lines of your pattern. It's very important to work within the shape (figure 3).

As you work, check your beadwork against the metal cuff to make sure that it fits. If you've stitched too tightly, you may have lost ¼ inch (6 mm) or more. This happens occasionally, which is why we didn't cut the piece out in the beginning. Backstitch more beads where needed. When your beadwork is complete, carefully cut the excess foundation flush against the beadwork.

2 Roll a smooth layer of industrial-strength adhesive to the back side of the beadwork, staying ¼ inch (6 mm) away from the edges to allow for later stitching. Glue the beadwork to the top of the metal cuff.

▶ Finish

Single thread a needle and tie a knot at the end. Weave through the beadwork to bury the knot and exit at the edge of the cuff. Use 11° seed beads and magatamas to stitch a picot edge all the way around the cuff (figure 4).

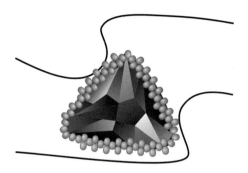

figure 1

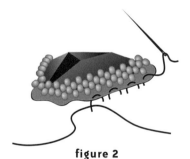

figure 2

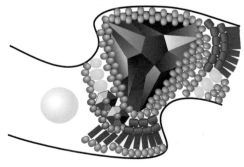

figure 3   **figure 4**

RHAPSODY EARRINGS

This design takes full advantage of the terrific variety of beads available today. The polka-dot and bright chartreuse daggers make a whimsical complement to the smooth glass cabochons.

Make 2

▶ Design and Embroider

1 Draw vertical and horizontal center lines on both pieces of beading foundation. Approximately ¼ inch (6 mm) above the center mark, attach the larger cabochon to the foundation with industrial-strength adhesive and allow it to dry.

2 Backstitch an even number of cylinder beads around the cabochon. From your backstitched row, work a few rows of peyote stitch with cylinder beads to form a bezel around the cabochon. When the bezel begins to flare out slightly, stitch a final row of 15°s to close up the top. Backstitch a row of the cylinder beads around the entire bezeled cabochon.

continued on next page

SUPPLIES

Basic Supplies (page 13)

Focal beads:
    1 light green round glass cabochon, 14–16 mm
    1 purple round glass cabochon, 6–8mm

Size 11° metallic green/gold iris cylinder beads, 3 g

Size 15° metallic gold seed beads, 5 g

10 bright blue AB bicone crystals, 4 mm

2 bright blue AB crystal sequins, 4 mm

8 black with green polka-dot dagger beads, 14 mm

4 chartreuse dagger beads, 9 mm

2 pieces of beading foundation, each 3 x 3 inches (7.6 x 7.6 cm)

2 pieces of suede, 3 x 3 inches each (7.6 x 7.6 cm)

2 gold lever-back ear wires

3 Glue the smaller cabochon on the vertical line below the large cabochon, flush against the backstitched ring of cylinder beads, using industrial-strength adhesive. Allow the glue to dry.

4 Backstitch a row of 15°s around the smaller cabochon from one side to the other. Gluing the stone flush against the larger cabochon will prevent you from stitching around the entire stone.

5 Backstitch bicones in the corners between the two cabochons. Backstitch a row of 15°s around the bicones to tie the entire piece together visually.

6 Use stop stitch to add a sequin centered between the cabochons

▶ Finish

1 Tie off your thread on the back with simple knots and clip the thread. Carefully cut the excess foundation flush against the beadwork and glue the beadwork to the suede with white glue. Allow this to dry, then cut the excess suede flush against the beadwork.

2 Thread a needle with 16 inches (40.6 cm) of thread. Begin at the top where the ear wire will be attached and stitch a single-bead edging with cylinder beads around the entire design.

▶ Attach the Ear Wire

1 Locate the top 3 center edge beads and pass the needle through one of the beads on either side of the center bead. Pick up four 15°s, the ear wire, and four 15°s. Pass the needle down through the edge bead on the opposite side of the center bead. Repeat the thread path, for strength.

2 Weave through the beads in the earring and tie off several small knots. Clip close.

▶ Fringe

Single or double thread your needle and pass it down through the bottom edge beads. Create a random fringe using 15°s, cylinders, bicones, and daggers. Have some fun with this—they don't have to match perfectly if you don't want them to. If you used single thread and your fringe is heavy, go back through the fringe twice, for strength.

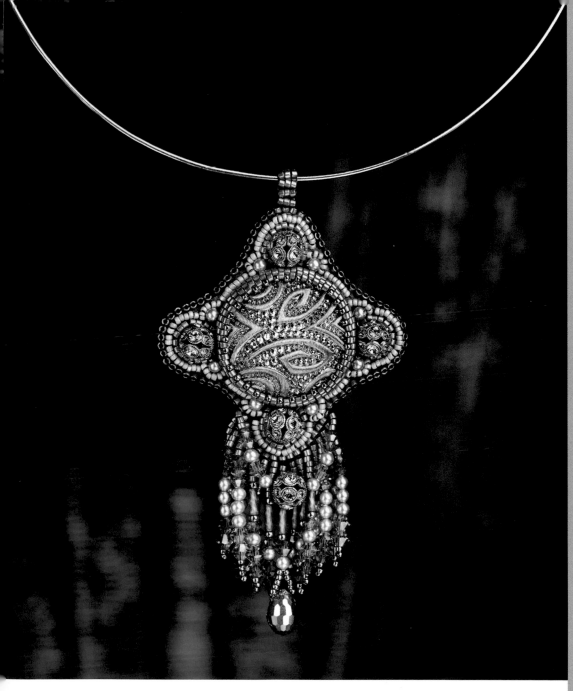

SUPPLIES

Basic Supplies (page 13)

Focal bead:
    28-mm button
    in gold tones

Size 11° metallic gold or bronze cylinder beads, 8 g

Size 15° seed beads:
    Metallic gold or bronze, 5 g
    Matte gold, 3 g

5 gold and warm jewel-tone filigree beads, 8 mm

40–50 gold or cream faux pearls, 2 mm

34–40 topaz bicone crystals, 3 mm

31–35 warm rose bicone crystals, 4 mm

5-mm gold tone bugle beads, 2 g

5 x 7 mm gold-tone crystal drop

Beading foundation, 4 x 4 inches (10 x 10 cm)

Poster board, 4 x 4 inches (10 x 10 cm)

Suede, 4 x 4 inches (10 x 10 cm)

1 gold neck ring (or any type desired)

Wire cutters

MILLION DOLLAR BABY PENDANT

This piece is all about a gorgeous button and stunning filigree beads. The symmetrical pendant can be hung from any type of neckband, and you can create a smaller version to make matching earrings.

figure 1

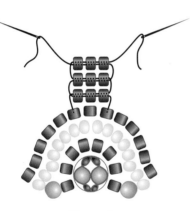

figure 2

▶ Embroider the Pendant

1 Cut the shank off the button and glue it with industrial-strength adhesive to the center of your beading foundation. Allow it to dry.

2 Thread your needle with 1 yard (94.1 cm) of thread and tie a knot. Backstitch an even number of cylinder beads around the button. From the backstitched row, work a few rows of even count peyote stitch with cylinder beads, forming a bezel. When the bezel begins to flare, stitch a final row with 15°s to close up around the button.

3 Mark the compass points around the bezeled button on your beading foundation. Backstitch 4 of the filigree beads, on at each of the compass points, flush against the bezeled button.

4 Backstitch 15° beads around the filigree beads, then backstitch the pearls in the 8 corners near the filigree beads (your work should look like figure 1).

5 Backstitch with 15°s around the entire design. Weave the thread to the back of the piece, tie off the threads, and clip close. Carefully cut the foundation flush against the beadwork.

6 Place the beadwork on the poster board and trace around it. Cut out the poster board ⅛ inch (3 mm) smaller than the beadwork and attach it to the back of the beadwork with white glue. Allow the glue to dry.

7 Attach the beadwork to the suede using white glue, and allow it to dry. Cut the suede flush against the beadwork.

► Finish

1 Single thread a needle with 18 inches (45.7) cm of thread and tie a knot. Bury the knot near the edge of the beadwork, under some beads, and exit at the edge of the beadwork. Stitch single-bead edging with the cylinder beads all the way around your beadwork. When your last bead meets your first, attach the two and weave the needle and thread back down through the beadwork, tie off several knots, and clip the thread close.

2 Locate the 3 top center edge beads on your pendant. This pendant is very symmetrical; if you can't find a centered set of 3 beads on one point, check another point and work from there. Thread 2 needles and anchor the threads in the beadwork. Pass one needle through the right edge bead and pass the other needle through the left edge bead. Create a 2-needle, ladder stitched bail by picking up 3 cylinder beads with the right needle and passing through them with the left needle (figure 2); continue until the bail is long enough to go around your chosen neck ring. Weave the working threads through the same edge beads from which you started the bail, then weave through those beads three more times for strength. Weave the threads through the beadwork, tie off several knots, and clip the threads.

► Fringe

1 Thread 1 yard (94.1 cm) of thread onto 2 needles to work double-needle fringe, beginning at the center edge bead on the lower point. You may follow my pattern (figure 3) or choose your own.

2 With the needles exiting downward through the edge beads next to the outer rows of fringe, string the loop that swoops across the front of the fringe. Pick up the beads for the loop (figure 4) with one of the needles and pass up through the edge bead on the opposite side of the fringe. Pass the other needle through the strand from the opposite direction.

3 String the pendant onto your neck wire or create a special beaded chain.

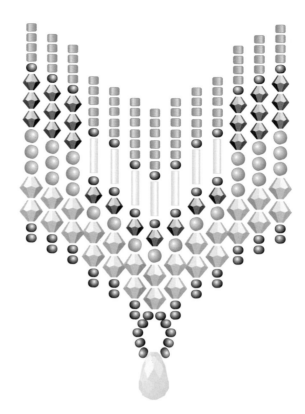

figure 3

figure 4

SUPPLIES

continued from previous page

Round crystal pendants:

> 1 gross of copper/slate round crystal pendants, 5 mm

> 1 gross of copper/slate round crystal pendants, 8 mm

15–25 gunmetal vintage nail heads, 4 mm

1 smoky quartz crystal teardrop, 30 x 50 mm or larger

2 olive crystal drops, 18 x 9 mm

2 pieces of beading foundation, 8½ x11 inches (21.6 x 27.9 cm)

2 pieces of poster board, 8½ x11 inches (21.6 x 27.9 cm)

26-gauge wire, six 4-inch (10 cm) lengths

Suede, 16 x 22 inches (40.6 x 55.9 cm)

2 silver-colored hook-and-eye sets

Chain nose pliers

Round nose pliers

Wire cutters

8-pound (3.6 k) test braided beading thread

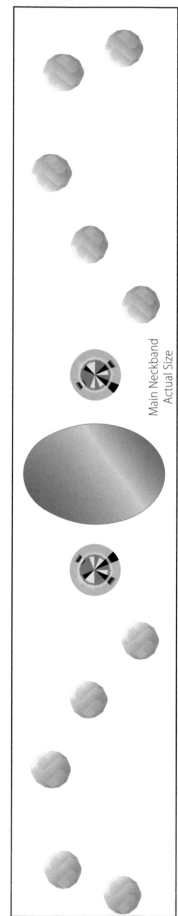

Main Neckband Actual Size

Back Neck Section Actual Size

Back Neck Section Actual Size

2 Trace the patterns onto beading foundation but don't cut them out. Use wire cutters to cut the shank off the button. Using industrial-strength adhesive, glue the button to the center of your neckband foundation, and then glue all of the cabochons in place on all 4 pieces of foundation, using my templates as a guide or creating your own design. Allow the glue on all components to dry.

3 Thread a needle with 1 yard (94.1 cm) of thread and tie a knot. Backstitch (page 17) an even number of cylinder beads around the oval button. From the backstitched row, work several rows of even-count peyote stitch with cylinder beads around the button, creating a bezel. When the bezel begins to flare out, stitch a final row with 15°s to close the top (page 19).

4 Repeat step 3 around all the cabochons.

▶ Embroider

1 Ready to spend lots of time being creative? Let's get started. It doesn't matter which piece you start with. For the main neckband, start at the center button and work out to the ends. I like to bead embroider a symmetrical piece

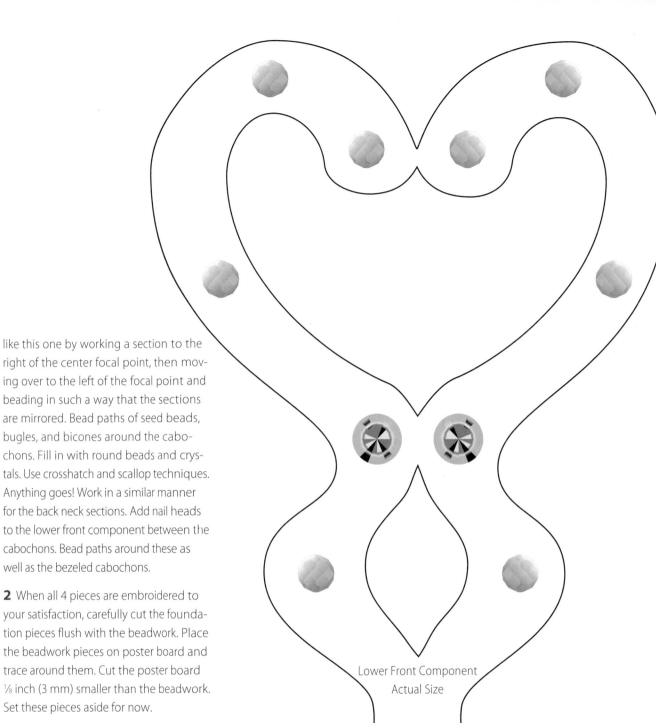

like this one by working a section to the right of the center focal point, then moving over to the left of the focal point and beading in such a way that the sections are mirrored. Bead paths of seed beads, bugles, and bicones around the cabochons. Fill in with round beads and crystals. Use crosshatch and scallop techniques. Anything goes! Work in a similar manner for the back neck sections. Add nail heads to the lower front component between the cabochons. Bead paths around these as well as the bezeled cabochons.

2 When all 4 pieces are embroidered to your satisfaction, carefully cut the foundation pieces flush with the beadwork. Place the beadwork pieces on poster board and trace around them. Cut the poster board ⅛ inch (3 mm) smaller than the beadwork. Set these pieces aside for now.

▶ Wire Connectors

1 Because of the weight of this large piece, wire is used to connect the neckband pieces, for added strength. **Note:** You may want to practice this on scrap wire first. Use your fingers and chain-nose pliers to straighten all of the wire

continued on next page

Lower Front Component
Actual Size

pieces. Using the same pliers, 1¼ inches (3.2 mm) from the end one of the wires, bend a right angle (figure 1). Position the jaws of the round nose pliers in the bend and use your fingers to curve the short end of the wire over the top jaw part of the round nose pliers (figure 2). Reposition the round nose pliers so the lower jaw fits into the loop snugly (figure 3). Create wraps by winding the shorter part of the wire around the stem with your fingers another 3 or 4 times (figure 4). Snip the excess wire with wire cutters and press the sharp end against the wraps with chain nose pliers, so it doesn't stick out.

2 Put one 3-mm Czech bead, one 11°, one 4-mm round crystal, one 11°, and one 3-mm Czech bead on the end of the wire. Create a loop on the other end of the wire, bending the wire at the right angle ¼ inch (6 mm) away from the beads, to accommodate the wraps. After wrapping, cut the excess wire and press it against the wraps, as before.

3 Repeat steps 1 and 2 on the remaining 5 pieces of wire.

▶ Connect the Neckband Pieces

1 Place the main neckband on your work surface with the two back pieces on either side of it, beadwork side down. Put a wire connector ¼ inch (6 mm) from the top edges between the main neckband and one of the back pieces, with the loops against the beading foundation and the strand of beads between the pieces. Mark the loop placement with a permanent marker. Measure ½ inch (1.3 cm) down and mark the placement for the second loop, then another ½ inch (1.3 cm) down for the last loop. Repeat for the other back piece.

2 Stitch the wires in place through the beadwork, hiding the stitches between the beads. Stitch the hook-and-eye closures in place, ¼ inch (6 mm) down from the top and ¼ inch (6 mm) up from the bottom (figure 5).

▶ Finish

1 Slightly curve the piece of poster board cut for the main neckband by rolling a pencil or dowel over the piece, much as you would to curl a piece of ribbon. Attach the cut pieces of poster board to the

figure 1

figure 2

figure 3

figure 4

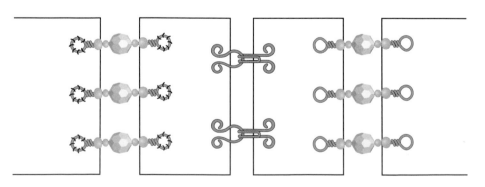

figure 5

backs of the beadwork pieces with white glue. (The poster board adds support to the pieces and covers the wires.) Allow the glue to dry, then attach suede to the backs of the beadwork pieces with white glue and allow it to dry.

2 Thread a needle with 18 inches (45.7 cm) of single thread and tie a knot at the end.

Bury the knot near the edge of the beadwork, under some beads, and exit at the edge of the beadwork. Stitch a single-bead edging with 11° B beads all the way around the main neckband. When your last bead meets your first, attach the two and weave the needle and thread back down through the beadwork, tie off several knots, and clip the thread close.

3 Repeat step 2 for all remaining pieces of beadwork. You'll have to maneuver a little bit to get around the pieces with the wire connectors and hook-and-eye closures.

continued on next page

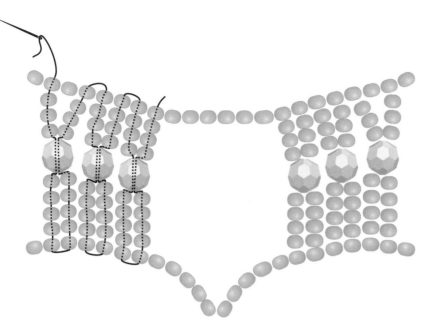

figure 6

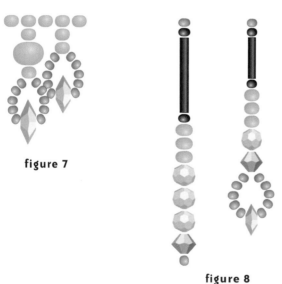

figure 7

figure 8

▶ Attach the Pieces

1 Measure about 1 inch (2.5 cm) to the right and to the left from the center of the focal button. These will be the starting points. Thread two needles with 1 yard (94.1 cm) of braided beading thread folded in half to create double threads, and tie knots at the ends. Weave through the beadwork and the foundation to bury the knots and add strength, and exit through the edge beads at the measured starting points.

2 Pick up three 11° As, one 4-mm round, and three 11° As. Weave through the corresponding edge bead at the top of the lower front component, stitch through the foundation for added strength, then pass through the next edge bead. Pick up three 11°s, pass through the 4-mm round, pick up three 11°s, and pass the needle up through the edge bead next to the edge bead first exited. Work 3 to 4 more netted sections to connect the components. Because of the curve along the top of the lower component, you may need to increase or decrease a seed bead on the other netted sections to accommodate the space or skip over an edge bead to make the piece hang correctly (figure 6). Pass through all of the netted sections again, for strength. Weave the needles through the beadwork, tie off several knots, and clip the thread close.

▶ Fringe

Note: Because you're working with crystals and heavy fringe, either use doubled thread or pass through all the fringe twice, for strength. My fringe is random but worked on both sides at the same time to ensure that the two sides are symmetrical.

1 Thread two needles to work both sides of the neckband. Weave through the beadwork to bury the knots and exit the edge beads on either side of the netted connectors. String one fringe on the right, and then mirror the same fringe on the left. My fringe on the neckband is a series of loops of 11° As, 15° As, 4-mm Czech beads, and 6-mm crystal pendants at the front and then 11° As, 15° As, and 5-mm crystal pendants toward the back (figure 7). Continue until the entire lower edge of the neckband is fringed.

2 The lower front component uses bugles, 11° seed beads, bicone crystals, round crystals, Czech beads, and round iridescent beads. The shortest bugles are used for the upper part of the component, transitioning to the medium length. The longest bugles are used for the middle part of the component, and the medium length are used again at the bottom. While the fringe is worked randomly and changes from section to section, all of them remain visually similar because each fringe begins the same way: one 11° B followed by one 11° A. As with the neckband, work both sides simultaneously to ensure even counts on both sides. See figure 8 for sample fringes. Place one of the smaller crystal drops in the center of the lowest fringe; how to do so is explained in the next section.

▶ Drops

1 Adding the large drop pendant in the center will be a challenge because of its weight. Thread a needle with doubled braided beading thread and tie a knot at the end. Weave through the beadwork to bury the knot into the foundation for added strength. Exit an edge bead near the top center of the top cutout. Pick up the desired number of beads to accommodate your pendant. I have two 15° As, one 4-mm round bead, eight 15° Bs, the pendant, and eight 15° Bs. Pass back through the 4-mm bead, pick up two 15° As, and pass through the corresponding edge bead on the other side of the cutout. Repeat the thread path at least once more for strength. Further embellish above the drop with seed beads and bicones as desired.

2 Add the small drop below the neckband focal bead in the same manner.

GALLERY

To show you the infinite variations possible with a technique as versatile as bead embroidery, I've included this gallery of adornments—and a few non-jewelry items—made by other artists. These photos demonstrate how big an impact your choice of focal bead or fun beads can make.

Reverse (clasp)

FAR LEFT

Diane Hyde

Tangled Up in Time, 2010

26.7 x 15 x 2 cm

Vintage watch parts and gears, two working watches, crystal bicones, glass pearls, seed beads, 4-mm cube beads, brass stampings, bead cord, wire, nylon thread, Ultrasuede backing, small hooks, beading foundation; bead embroidered, picot edging, stringing

PHOTOS BY ARTIST

TOP

Heidi Kummli

Transformation, 2008

30.5 x 17.8 x 1.3 cm

Various materials; bead embroidered

PHOTO BY ARTIST

BOTTOM

Heidi Kummli

Polar Bear Bracelet, 2010

5.1 x 17.8 x 2.5 cm

Toy, cast animals, various stones; bead embroidered

PHOTO BY ARTIST

TOP

Jean Forquer Hyslop

Frames, 2009

26 x 18 x 0.2 cm

Peyote bezels, crystal frames, pearls, seed beads, cabochon by Gary Wilson, semi-precious embellishment beads, Ultrasuede backing; bead embroidered

PHOTO BY BLAIR DAVIS

BOTTOM LEFT

Yoli Pastuszak

Encrusted Ammonite, 2008

9 x 5.1 x 0.8 cm

Seed beads, ammonite cabochon, crystals, freshwater pearls, Lacy's Stiff Stuff, brass cuff blank; bead embroidered, even-count peyote, fringe stitch

PHOTO BY MARGIE DEEB

BOTTOM RIGHT

Yoli Pastuszak

Stingray, 2010

9 x 5.08 x .75 cm

Seed beads, mammoth ivory netsuke, abalone beads, Czech fire-polished beads, beading foundation, brass cuff blank; bead embroidered

PHOTO BY MARGIE DEEB

Dixie Gabric

Welcome to My Web, 2009

48.3 x 43.2 cm

Pearls, stone cabochon, seed beads, triangles, hex beads, bugles, charm; backstitch, peyote, layering, edging

PHOTO BY JERRY ANTHONY

BOTTOM LEFT AND RIGHT

Laurie Danch

Cupid Collar, 2006

22 x 18 x 2 cm

Brass stamping, abalone, pearls, crystals, seed beads; peyote, backstitch

PHOTOS BY MARTIN KONOPACKI

OTHER BOOKS IN THIS SERIES

Diane Fitzgerald's Shaped Beadwork

Along with color, texture, and luminosity, shape can set a piece of jewelry apart. This renowned beading teacher shows you how to weave simple increase patterns to make beautiful two- and three-dimensional forms. Some of the projects consist of creating a single bead in a specific shape; most of the projects offer instructions for making complete pieces of jewelry. The versatile patterns Diane provides are building blocks that you can use to design your own jewelry.

Diane Fitzgerald received the 2008 Bead & Button Show Excellence in Bead Artistry Award. She has authored numerous books devoted to beads and beadwork.

Marcia DeCoster's Beaded Opulence

Right angle weave is an essential, versatile stitch for creating fantastic beadwork. Marcia DeCoster presents more than 20 magnificent adornments to make using this stitch. Marcia's skill-building projects teach you how to create supple beaded fabric, beaded ropes, shaped curves, and embellished layers. Complete with an inspiring gallery of right angle weave work by other artists, this beautifully photographed book will enable you to make spectacular jewelry of eye-catching complexity.

Marcia DeCoster's work has been featured in many leading magazines and publications. She teaches workshops in the United States and internationally.

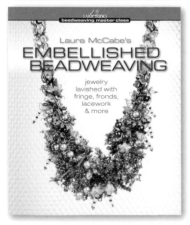

Laura McCabe's Embellished Beadweaving

Laura McCabe begins by taking you through basics stitches and techniques. Then she provides directions for a variety of lovely embellishment forms inspired by flora, fauna, art nouveau, and geometric forms. Finally, she gives you 18 opulent jewelry designs to put your skills to use. Complete with advice on approaching color and design, this book gives you a solid foundation for developing your own unique pieces.

Laura McCabe shows her jewelry in both national and international beadwork exhibitions and teaches workshops in the United States as well as around the globe.